A Reading of Villon's *Testament*

A READING OF VILLON'S *TESTAMENT*

By

David A. Fein

Summa Publications, Inc.
Birmingham, Alabama
1984

Copyright 1984
Summa Publications, Inc.
ISBN 0-917786-04-1
Library of Congress Catalog Card Number 84-050322
Printed in the United States of America

FRONTISPIECE

CONTENTS

Preface

I have always found teaching François Villon's *Testament* to be a rewarding if sometimes frustrating experience. For the students, I suspect, the experience has often been more frustrating than rewarding. Although they may find themselves attracted to the beauty of certain intensely lyrical moments of the poem, and fascinated by the personality they sense behind the mask of sarcasm and irony, they must continually struggle against formidable obstacles of language if they are to find any degree of clarity and coherency in this complex work. The difficulties confronting an uninitiated twentieth-century reader of the *Testament* derive not only from the unfamiliar nature of fifteenth-century French, but also from Villon's frequently contorted syntax, his masterful use of ambiguous language, and the wealth of historical, Biblical, and autobiographical allusions.

It is small wonder that students or even teachers of French not specializing in the medieval period often feel overwhelmed by the task of deciphering this enigmatic text. A substantial body of scholarship on the *Testament* is now available, but the variety of critical approaches and the divergent interpretations that may be found for any passage of the poem only serve to further bewilder the perplexed reader. It has often occurred to me while teaching the *Testament* that a concise analysis of certain key passages tracing the broadest thematic lines of the poem would be useful to both students and teachers trying to make some sense out of this baffling work of art.

The passages of the poem that I have selected for discussion are those I have found most interesting to teach, and which students seem most inclined to explore. They are linked by certain thematic threads that run throughout the poem--mortality, suffering, spiritual transcendence, for example. My own approach to the *Testament*, one I am sure I share with other readers, is posited on a belief that the poem's framework, namely its testamentary form, ought to be taken seriously. I consider the work to be more than a dazzling carnival, an extravagant farce. Although an element of spectacle and mockery undeniably exists, the poem reflects a personal drama whose development I have attempted to trace. From the awareness of mortality evident in the first verse to the seemingly flippant funeral oration of the closing ballad, the *Testament* unfolds under the shadow of death. Like any actual will of the fifteenth century, the work possesses a strong religious character.

The scene reproduced in the frontispiece is taken from Guyot Marchant's *Danse Macabre*, published in 1485. Like the other drawings in Marchant's edition, this picture is generally believed to have been copied from the mural representing the dance of death on the walls of the Innocents, the well known Parisian cemetery mentioned in the *Testament*. The scene dramatically illustrates the familiarity with which Villon's contemporaries regarded death. So central is the role of death to the late medieval conception of life, that it is difficult to imagine a profound artistic work of the period that does not in some way confront what is perhaps the most basic of all human fears.

That the *Testament* is witty, clever, ironic is indisputable, and a large portion of current criticism rightly emphasizes these facets of the poem. Yet it is not the poet's wittiness, cleverness, or irony that endows the work with its depth, its universality, its almost haunting quality. To draw closer to the source of the *Testament*'s enduring character, one must explore its spiritual dimensions. This aspect of the work has always fascinated and mystified me. I remain convinced that whatever intriguing digressions and distractions the *Testament* may contain, its deepest significance lies in the troubling questions it raises concerning philosophical values.

A considerable number of erudite studies, each in its own way a valuable contribution, have been written on Villon. For example, there are books relating his work to medieval literary tradition and medieval scholasticism, others that explore the semantic richness of his work or provide a philological analysis of his poetry in a verse-by-verse commentary. What has been lacking, however, is a book-length study that presents a reading of the *Testament*, tracing the development of its dominant thematic patterns without isolating these patterns from the organic unity of the poem. This is, in my opinion, simply a case of not being able to see the forest for the trees. Villon's *Testament*, which surely must rank among the most difficult poems written in the French language, demands close range attention in order to clarify obscure passages and unravel stubborn verbal knots. But to be fully appreciated as a work of art, it also must be viewed from a distance adequate to reveal its broadest thematic lines.

A Reading of Villon's Testament could serve as the title to numerous interpretations of the poem, each one different from the next, and it would be foolish and presumptuous indeed to claim that this particular study presents the definitive interpretation of Villon's poem. My primary purpose is simply to invite my readers--students, teachers, even Villon scholars--to consider one possible (although perhaps unorthodox) reading of the *Testament*. If this little book succeeds in causing the reader to ponder even a small portion of the poem, to find a new meaning in it, or perhaps, thoughtfully responding to the proposed interpretation, to affirm or reaffirm a meaning very different from the one suggested, then this study will have achieved its modest objective.

Villon's poem may be read on at least three different levels. The first layer of meaning might be termed the "surface value" of the text, i.e., that which Villon appears to be saying. Given the poet's penchant for sarcasm and irony, one must obviously approach the surface value cautiously and critically. On the other hand, it would be unwise to dismiss out of hand every statement that Villon makes, on the assumption that the truth is always to be found beneath a disguise of sincerity. When Villon states his age, recalls his recent imprisonment, speaks of his poverty, or eloquently portrays the simplicity of his mother's faith, we have no cause to probe beneath his words for his "real" meaning. To ignore the self-evident truth of these assertions would result in a poor reading if not a misreading of the passages in question. The second layer of meaning, the most pervasive and consequently the most extensively studied, consists of masking the truth under an obvious travesty. When Villon speaks of his enemies with benevolence or praise, he clearly means the opposite of what he says. While one should be cognizant of Villon's tendency to playfully conceal his true intention beneath deceitful language, the patterns formed by the choice of subterfuge, for example those treated in the sixth chapter, are also worthy of attention. The third level on which the poem may be read is that of symbolic meaning. The acrostic signature found in his mother's prayer to the Virgin and in the "Ballade de la Grosse Margot," the state of nudity to which we see the poet reduced on several occasions, the image of snow in Villon's most famous ballad, the inscription he leaves as an epitaph, all are invested with significant symbolic value.

To read the *Testament* straight through at only one of these three levels would violate the poem's integrity as a multi-layered composite of meaning. The task of the reader, one which the intimidating complexity of the *Testament* does not facilitate, is to locate a strand of continuity and then trace its progress as it weaves through the various layers of the poem. The nine essays that follow represent one attempt to carry out this task, and to thus arrive at a tentative understanding of Villon's masterpiece.

Given the nature of this study and the primary audience for which it is intended, I have made an effort to limit the footnotes to observations which I consider essential. In the notes I have included occasional explanations relating to quotations from the *Testament*, as well as indications of secondary sources that the reader may wish to consult in connection with a given passage or aspect of the poem. A selected bibliography has been included to acquaint the reader with the most useful contributions to the rapidly growing body of scholarship on Villon's work. Although the present study is not principally directed toward a scholarly audience, it is my hope that Villon scholars may find a few new ideas here. The study is intended to do more than simply rehash existing interpretations of the *Testament*.

In order to keep discussion of the poem from becoming too abstract, I have found it useful to quote generously from Villon's poem. Because of the linguistic difficulties facing the unitiated reader of the *Testament*, I have chosen to provide translations for all passages quoted from the poem. These English excerpts are taken from Galway Kinnell's translation of the Longnon-Foulet text. Some readers may find Kinnell's lack of punctuation slightly annoying, and I was occasionally tempted to insert a comma or period where one seemed appropriate, but refrained from altering his translation in any way. Although I admit reservations concerning Kinnell's treatment of certain passages, I find that his rendition of the poem is the English translation that comes closest to the French text. On the few occasions where I feel his interpretation may be misleading, I have inserted an explanatory note for the purpose of clarification.

The seminal stages of this study first appeared in *Fifteenth-Century Studies* and *Neophilologus*. The University of North Carolina at Greensboro generously supported this work by granting me a research leave in the fall of 1982, as well as a Research Council award in the following year. I wish to express my gratitude to Professor Wallace Fowlie, whose profound admiration of Villon I share, for his interest, guidance, and kind words of encouragement. I also wish to thank Professor Norris J. Lacy, Editor of Summa Publications, for his cooperation and assistance. For her invaluable moral support, I am, as always, deeply grateful to my wife Rita.

CHAPTER ONE: THE PRELUDE (Verses 1-224)

The *Testament* opens with a bitter memory, the poet's recent experience in the prison of Thibaut d'Aussigny, bishop of Orléans:[1]

> En l'an de mon trentiesme aage,
> Que toutes mes hontes j'eus beues,
> Ne du tout fol, ne du tout sage,
> Non obstant maintes peines eues,
> Lesquelles j'ay toutes receues
> Soubz la main Thibault d'Aussigny.

> (In my thirtieth year of life
> When I had drunk down all of my disgrace
> Neither altogether a fool nor altogether wise
> Despite the many blows I had
> Every one of which I took
> At Thibault d'Aussigny's hand).[2]

At the moment of writing the *Testament* the poet exists in a state of limbo. First, he is neither a prisoner nor a truly free man.[3] At the age of thirty, although not yet actually old, he has clearly, both by medieval standards of longevity and his own perception, moved beyond the realm of youth. As he states in the third verse, his mind can neither be described as foolish nor wise. Reliving the suffering of his imprisonment, he hovers somewhere between the present and the past. Finally, like any religiously instructed man of the fifteenth century, he wavers dangerously at every moment between salvation and perdition. Transcending all of these ambivalent states is the ultimate uncertainty, the ambiguous and mysterious region of time immediately preceding death. Adopting the pose of a dying man, Villon places the *Testament* in a sort of no man's land between life and death, an ideal setting for this deeply equivocal poem.

One might reasonably expect a testamentary document to begin with some mention of a date and a reference to the identity of the testator. Villon's *Lais*, in fact, opens precisely in this fashion:

> L'an quatre cens cinquante six,
> Je, Françoys Villon, escollier (1-2)

> (In the year fourteen fifty-six
> I the scholar François Villon).

The *Testament*, by contrast, immediately plunges us into an inner world where time is measured in personal terms:

> En l'an de mon trentiesme aage.

The dating of a will gives the document a certain validity, a sense of coherence, tying it firmly and logically to the world that will survive the testator. The "dating" of the *Testament*, instead of placing the text in a historical context, situates it squarely within a personal chronology. The poem's year of composition, 1461, does surface eventually (and almost incidentally) some eighty verses later. Historical authenticity, as we see from the opening verse, has been relegated to a position of secondary importance. The fact that the poem was written in 1461 is not judged by Villon as central to its meaning. The poet's age, on the other hand, is deemed significant enough to be revealed immediately.

The fourth decade of human life, especially the early thirties, is traditionally associated with some sort of momentous event, frequently of a religious nature. It was at this age that Jesus began preaching and attracting followers, that Augustine converted to Christianity, that Dante undertook his imaginary journey. A more recent example is Pascal, whose famous religious experience occurred when he was thirty-one. We can only speculate on the importance Villon attaches to his age, but we need not look far into his past to find an influential experience. Of all the recollections that surface in the course of the poem, it is the memory of the bishop's prison, still fresh and painful, that dominates. Villon's personal acquaintance with physical and psychological suffering will be felt throughout the poem. It is difficult to escape the feeling that the poet's newly acquired experience has in some way profoundly affected his existence. As he himself states later in the poem:

> Travail mes lubres stentemens,
> Esguisez comme une pelote,
> M'ouvrit plus que tous les *Commens*
> D'Averroÿs sur Aristote. (93-96)

> (Suffering unlocked my tangled feelings
> About as sharp as a ball of wool
> More than all the *Commentaries*
> of Averroes opened Aristotle).

It is not only his age that Villon places at the head of his poem, but also the memory that cannot be separated from that age. In approaching the *Testament*, we must keep in mind that the poem which will eventually undergo so many puzzling and grotesque transformations has its source in a thirty-year-old man's memory of a very painful and still very present experience.

The name of Thibault d'Aussigny in the opening stanza of the poem sets off a bitter invective occupying the next five stanzas. In sharp contrast to this vehement denunciation of the bishop, the next few stanzas sing the praises of the man responsible for Villon's release from prison, Louis XI.[4] Reflections on past wanderings and sufferings follow, leading the poet's thoughts to take a religious turn:

> Je suis pecheur, je le sçay bien;
> Pourtant ne veult pas Dieu ma mort,
> Mais convertisse et vive en bien
> Et tout autre que pechié mort. (105-108)

> (I am a sinner I know it well
> And yet God doesn't want me to die
> But to repent and live right
> And so with all others bitten by sin).

This passage merits attention, among other reasons, for the directness with which the poet speaks of himself. In a poem characterized by equivocal and often devious language, the bald assertion "Je suis pecheur" stands out forcefully. But can we take Villon at his word? A few moments ago he was telling us that he would pray for Thibault:

> Sy prieray pour luy de bon cuer (33)

> (So I'll pray for him gladly),

when he clearly had no such intention. Part of the charm and the difficulty of the *Testament* relates to its diversity of tones. Simply because sarcasm is a frequent tone, we cannot accurately infer that the entire poem is meant to be taken sarcastically. Nor does the heavy use of irony necessarily mean that all seemingly sincere assertions are undercut by hidden irony. It is, in fact, this unpredictable alternation between flippancy and seriousness that gives the poem so much of its unique character.

The question of sincerity poses considerable problems for the reader of the *Testament*.[5] How are we to know when to take Villon seriously? Some readers become so distrustful of the poet that they refuse to take any of his statements at face value. To deprive the poem of all sincerity and gravity, however, does an injustice to the work by limiting its richness of tone. Moreover, no serious critic would argue that the poem is devoid of any genuine emotion. Disagreement only arises over where and how the poet's feelings actually make themselves known. Ultimately, each reader must determine for himself how the poet means each stanza and ballad of his poem to be taken. In making this determination, the reader may find it useful to distinguish between the "voice" Villon typically uses when speaking of his relationship to others, especially his enemies--a mocking, hard-edged, contemptuous voice that clearly does not mean what it says--and the register he normally uses when reflecting on his own condition. The second tone is, by comparison, softer, less strident, more contemplative, easier to trust. When Villon tells us that he will pray for Thibault, we know immediately that his statement is suspect. When he tells us that he is a sinner, the veracity of his assertion can hardly be questioned.

From the small amount of precise biographical data we have on Villon's life prior to the composition of the *Testament*, it is evident that this young man was hardly a candidate for sainthood. But whatever specific transgressions the poet may have in mind when he confesses himself a sinner, the word *pecheur* universalizes his condition, linking him to the whole of humanity, which, according to Catholic doctrine, is inherently sinful.[6] The confession of sin here constitutes the first of a series of religious acts. Before the poem is finished, we will also witness an extended prayer, a brief requiem, and a mysterious act which may perhaps be best construed as eucharistic in nature.

Following a short anecdotal digression (the story of Alexander and Diomedes), the poet's thoughts turn again to his past:

> Je plains le temps de ma jeunesse,
> (Ouquel j'ay plus qu'autre gallé
> Jusques a l'entree de vieillesse),
> Qui son partement m'a celé. (169-172)

> (I mourn the days of my youth
> When more than most I had my fling
> Until age came upon me
> It gave me no warning it would leave).

Whether or not we accept his assertion that he has entered old age (or, to keep closer to the text, that old age has entered his life), Villon's clear intention is to present himself as irrevocably separated from his youth. The most apparent reason for assuming the identity of an old man is related to the fiction of the will. Villon claims at various points in the poem that he is sick, old, and weak, and therefore must turn his attention to the task at hand, the dictation of his will. The separation from youth, however, need not be taken as purely fictitious. Here and elsewhere in the poem, as Villon looks back nostalgically and regretfully on his past, he creates the impression of a man surveying his youth from a great distance. This time gap is altogether absent in the *Lais*, written five years earlier.

From memories of his youth, Villon returns to the present:

Allé s'en est, et je demeure,
Povre de sens et de savoir,
Triste, failly, plus noir que meure,
Qui n'ay ne cens, rente, n'avoir;
Des miens le mendre, je dis voir,
De me desavouer s'avance,
Oubliant naturel devoir
Par faulte d'ung peu de chevance. (177-184)

It* has gone and I stay on
Poor in sense and knowledge
Sad, sick, blacker than a mulberry
Without cents, rent, or goods
The last of my kin I speak the truth
Steps up to disown me
Forgetting their natural duty
For my lack of a bit of money).

*my youth

The word *povre*, appearing in the second verse, is a key adjective which Villon repeatedly applies to himself. In this stanza we see depicted a man who is poor in many ways. First, and most obviously, he lacks financial resources. But his poverty also extends into his mental, physical, and emotional resources. He lacks sense, happiness, and physical well-being. The picture is one of utter solitude, the solitude of a man abandoned by youth, fortune, and even by his own family. The profession of poverty, the confession of sin, and, later, the condition of nakedness combine to create an attitude of humility that contrasts strikingly with the vicious attacks Villon sporadically directs against his enemies. The fluctuation from contempt to humility, along with the attendant shift of tone, is only one of several patterns of alternation that endow the poem with a captivating sense of movement and rhythm.

Villon's description of himself as "plus noir que meure" may be read in various manners. If *failly* is taken to mean "weak" or "sick," then the phrase might be understood as describing a diseased complexion. The other sense of *failly*, "discouraged," would indicate a figurative interpretation-- "gloomy," "somber," and "pessimistic" would be the closest English equivalents. At a symbolic level, the color black carries two connotations which could apply here. Black has a long history of association with both death and sin. "Plus noir que meure" therefore simultaneously reminds us that the poem is allegedly the final discourse of a dying man, and serves as a symbolic restatement of Villon's recent confession, "Je suis pecheur." Black, the absence of all color, fittingly complements the other absences indicated in this stanza. Finally, this is the color of mourning, the appropriate color for a man grieving the loss of his youth, his happiness, and his family's support.

Continuing to lament his misspent youth, Villon speculates on how his present condition might now be different if he had pursued a different direction:

> Hé Dieu, se j'eusse estudié
> Ou temps de ma jeunesse folle
> Et a bonnes meurs dedié
> J'eusse maison et couche molle.
> Mais quoy? je fuyoie l'escolle,
> Comme fait le mauvais enfant.
> En escripvant ceste parolle
> A peu que le cuer ne me fent. (201-208)

> (Ah God if only I had studied
> In the days of my heedless youth
> And set myself in good ways
> I'd have a house now and soft bed
> But I ran from that school
> Like some good-for-nothing child
> As I write these words
> My heart is nearly breaking).

By dedicating himself to *bonnes meurs*, by simply conforming to the most basic social expectations, Villon might easily have achieved a minimal degree of material comfort. To some readers the stated desire for bourgeois security may seem irreconcilable with the rebellious character that incited Villon to commit his crimes. These readers may prefer to read the stanza as a tongue-in-cheek remark. Yet there is no internal evidence, no discernable clue to justify such a reading. Just because the financially prosperous are frequently targeted by Villon's devastating wit, it cannot be assumed that he rejects their style of life. On the contrary, one senses a hunger for comfort, a yearning for the ease of wealth on the part of a man well acquainted with poverty and deprivation.

In the next stanza a paraphrased quotation from Ecclesiastes stressing the ignorance of youth reinforces the poet's lament. The early section of the *Testament* is permeated with a sense of regret. From the more immediate memories of the prison at Meung, Villon moves deeper into his past. Mixed with regret is astonishment at the speed with which his life is passing:

> Mes jours s'en sont allez errant
> Comme, dit Job, d'une touaille
> Font les filetz, quant tisserant
> En son poing tient ardente paille:
> Lors, s'il y a nul bout qui saille,
> Soudainement il le ravit.
> Si ne crains plus que rien m'assaille,
> Car a la mort tout s'assouvit. (217-224)

> (My days have fled away
> Just as Job says the threads do
> On a cloth when the weaver
> Takes a burning straw in his hand
> Then if a stray end sticks out
> He razes it in a flash
> So I no longer fear what ills may come
> For everything finishes in death).

By paraphrasing Job, Villon identifies himself with the Biblical character. Like Job, Villon consistently portrays himself as a victim, and the theme of victimization, whether applying to Villon or to those who claim his sympathy, will resurface frequently in the poem. Like the Book of Job, the *Testament*, the Book of Villon, is very much concerned with the subject of suffering. Villon, however, has taken some liberties with the Biblical text. Job's statement reads simply: "My days are swifter than a weaver's shuttle."[7] By intensifying the emphasis on the brevity and fragility of human life, Villon creates a more graphic and more violent image, rich in meaning. His existence is merely a stray thread, a "bout qui saille," a defect in the cloth that must be eliminated. But the burning of the thread, far from an act of random violence, constitutes a purposeful act contributing to the perfection of the weaver's creation. Taken in this light, Villon's analogy clearly becomes a religious metaphor.

The last verse announces a series of meditations on death which will shortly follow. This stanza marks an important juncture in the poem. The memory of Meung, intimately associated with suffering and humiliation, leads through penitence to the confrontal of a wasted youth, eventually to a contemplation of the brevity of life, and finally to an awareness of the omnipotent destructive force of death. Suffering, sin, mortality--these are the major chords we will hear echoed throughout the *Testament*.

CHAPTER TWO: THE DANCE OF DEATH (Verses 225-412)

It is not until the twenty-ninth stanza that death makes its first dramatic appearance in the *Testament*:

> Ou sont les gracieux gallans
> Que je suivoye ou temps jadis,
> Si bien chantans, si bien parlans,
> Si plaisans en faiz et en dis?
> Les aucuns sont morts et roidis,
> D'eulx n'est il plus riens maintenant. (225-230)

> (Where are the happy young men
> I ran with in the old days
> Who sang so well, who spoke so well
> So excellent in word and deed?
> Some are stiffened in death
> And of those there's nothing left).

Contemplating the fate of his deceased comrades, Villon rehearses for the confrontation with his own death. As he followed them in his youth, so will he follow them again when his allotted time of life expires. The first four verses of the stanza possess a strongly musical cadence, giving the passage a refrain-like quality. Villon, in effect, takes up the song the *gallans* can no longer sing, for like them he is *biens chantans* and *bien parlans*. Rather than the physical appearance of the young men, it is their creative activities, especially those of a verbal nature, that attract the poet's attention. The verse "D'eulx n'est il plus riens" refers specifically to the physical remains of the *gallans*, that which death has stiffened. The young men's songs, words, and wit, their *diz*, however, have not been completely erased by death, but survive in the poet's memory. The question "mais ou sont les gracieux gallans?" announces the famous refrain "Mais ou sont les neiges d'antan?". Villon directly replies to the first question; the second will be left deliberately unanswered.

The *gallans* still living have encountered various fates. Some, according to Villon, have ended up as beggars, others as monks, while the most fortunate ones are now "grans seigneurs et maistres" (234). Villon, making little effort to disguise his envy, shows himself somewhat less than charitable toward the latter. His criticism of the *grans seigneurs* weakens, however, as he considers his own imperfections:

Je ne suis juge, ne commis
Pour pugnir n'absoudre mesfait:
De tous suis le plus imparfait,
Loué soit le doulx Jhesu Crist!
Que par moy leur soit satisfait!
Ce que j'ay escript est escript.[1] (259-264)

(I'm no judge nor a deputy
For pardoning or punishing wrongs
I'm the most imperfect of all
Praised be the mild Jesus Christ
Through me may they be satisfied
What I have written is written).

The theme of justice takes various forms in the *Testament*. First, we find numerous references to the civil and ecclesiastical judicial system with which, obviously, Villon was personally well acquainted. Echos of the Christian teachings on the fallibility of human justice, less frequent but equally important, may also be found in the poem, the most notable example occurring in the passage under discussion. Transcending the imperfect system of human justice, an awareness of divine justice manifests itself at sporadic intervals throughout the work. Finally, in spite of his assertion that he is not a judge, Villon cannot refrain from passing judgment, either implicitly or explicitly, on many of the figures who parade through the poem. Like Pilate, whom he quotes in the last verse of the stanza, he has the final authority in the little kingdom he "governs," the world of the *Testament*. Pilate's words when transferred to the context of Villon's poem emphasize the power of the written word, the capacity of the poet to order his world through verbal manipulation.

The verses quoted above contain a contradiction. On one hand, Villon admits his own imperfections and appears to disavow any harsh judgments he has rendered up to this point in the poem. On the other hand, he stubbornly refuses to retract his words, saying, "Ce que j'ay escript est escript." The reader who feels uncomfortable with this paradox may resolve the problem by claiming that Villon's admission of fallibility can be taken no more seriously than his "Je suis pecheur." Both, it might be argued, are simply farcical attempts at humility and piety. This explanation, however, neglects the fundamental fact that the *Testament*, like human nature itself, is full of contradictions. It is precisely this mass of oppositions that provides the inner tension necessary to sustain the poem's intensity through more than two thousand verses.

Before returning to the theme of death, Villon again expounds upon his destitute condition, depicting his poverty as a sort of family inheritance that can be traced to his ancestors. In times of despair, however, his heart comforts him with words of consolation:

> Homme, ne te doulouse tant
> Et ne demaine tel douleur,
> Se tu n'as tant qu'eust Jaques Cuer:
> Mieulx vault vivre soubz gros bureau
> Povre, qu'avoir esté seigneur
> Et pourrir soubz riche tumbeau! (283-288)

> (Man don't be so downhearted
> And carry on in such gloom
> Because you're not rich like Jacques Coeur
> Better to live under common cloth
> Poor, than having once been a lord
> To rot under an expensive tomb).

The word *povre*, adverbially linked to *vivre*, becomes an emblem of life, while *riche*, modifying *tumbeau*, becomes associated with death. The effect of this transposition of values is to bring into question the true meaning of wealth. If to be rich means to have an abundance of that which is truly precious, Villon's heart reminds him, then his financial poverty matters little compared to his incalculable wealth, the possession of a living body. Indeed one of the sharpest ironies of the *Testament* lies in the contrast between Villon's repeatedly stated poverty and the wealth of wit and intellectual energy that could only come from a man abounding with life.

Among the many conflicts of the *Testament*, the elemental struggle between life and death looms largest, a clash whose intensity is heightened by the fast approaching death of the poem's dying protagonist. It is important to bear in mind that while death figures prominently in the work, casting its shadow over practically all of the *Testament*, the affirmation of life is equally omnipresent, constantly contending with its negative counterpart. The tone of the poem is about to turn very grim. Now Villon, in a

preface to his lengthy meditation on mortality, asserts, and will reassert in
various ways throughout the remainder of the poem, that in the awesome face
of death he remains for the present very much alive.

   The specter of death, however, is never far away. The motif of the
danse macabre, the dance of death, surfaces shortly after Villon's
expression of gratitude for being alive. Here we see figures representing all
physical, social, and moral conditions united and equalized by their
common fate:

> Je congnois que povres et riches,
> Sages et folz, prestres et laiz,
> Nobles, villains, larges et chiches,
> Petitz et grans, et beaulx et laiz,
> Dames a rebrassez colletz,
> De quelconque condicion,
> Portans atours et bourreletz,
> Mort saisit sans excepcion. (305-312)

> (I know that the poor and the rich
> The wise and the foolish, the priests and the laymen
> The nobles, the serfs, the generous, the mean
> Small and great, handsome and ugly
> Ladies in upturned collars
> No matter what their rank
> Whether in kerchiefs or *bourrelets*[2]
> Death seizes them without exception).

The visual representation of the *danse macabre*, which served as a model
for the poetic description, was a common sight for Parisians of Villon's day,
the most famous example being the mural that decorated the cloister walls
in the Cemetery of the Innocents.[3] The artistic motif depicts a circle of
dancers representing every rung of the social and religious hierarchy,
following a grinning skeleton who leads the dance. Just as the eye must
move over the entire chain of dancers before finally arriving at the
skeleton, so the reader must view all the figures presented by Villon before
encountering the personification of death. The placement of the word *Mort*
proves especially strategic: death is literally waiting at the end. *Mort* gives
grammatical meaning to the preceding verses, just as death gives philosophical

and religious meaning to all that precedes it. "Mort saisit" appropriately breaks the rhythm of the dance which has been steadily building in intensity. The *Testament*, like the *danse macabre*, embraces all human conditions from prostitution to sainthood, joining them together in a dramatic dance, sometimes graceful, sometimes grotesque, and always moving, in both senses of the word.

Not content to leave death in the realm of abstraction with the phrase "Mort saisit sans excepcion," Villon goes on to present several graphic illustrations of the physical suffering often associated with the act of dying:

> Et meure Paris ou Helaine,
> Quiconques meurt, meurt a douleur
> Telle qu'il pert vent et alaine;
> Son fiel se creve sur son cuer,
> Puis sue, Dieu scet quelle sueur! (313-317)

> (Be it Paris or Helen who dies
> Whoever dies dies in such pain
> The wind is knocked out of him
> His gall breaks on his heart
> And he sweats God knows what sweat).

Paris and Helen, the first of a series of paired lovers to appear in the poem, serve most immediately to illustrate the degrading ravages of death which even the most perfect human specimens must endure. Villon could have chosen any number of archetypal lovers; it is not by accident that these two lead the parade of unhappy lovers, Villon among them, who will wander through the *Testament*. If the first association brought to mind by their names is beauty, the second must be violence, for their illicit relationship was the cause of a catastrophic war. Paris and Helen are in fact inseparable from the Trojan War, without which their union would be prosaic and unexceptional. In the context of the *Testament* Paris becomes the first of the martyrs of love. His death, provoked by an arrow wound received during the war, parallels the death of the martyred Villon, wounded, as we are told at the end of the poem, by the arrow of Love.

After inserting a comment on the solitary nature of the act of dying, Villon continues in even more graphic detail his description of the agony of death:

La mort le fait fremir, pallir,
Le nez courber, les vaines tendre,
Le col enfler, la chair mollir,
Joinctes et nerfs croistre et estendre. (321-324)

(Death makes him shudder and blanch
Makes the nose curve, the veins tighten
The neck puff, the flesh go limp
The joints and sinews swell and stretch).

Little is left to the reader's imagination as he is bluntly, almost brutally confronted with the physical agony of death. While the late medieval mentality shows a peculiar fascination with death and dying, few literary passages can rival this unflinching contemplation of the final tortuous moments of human life. The high concentration of verbs (eight within four verses) helps to create a vivid picture of active suffering, allowing us to visualize the dying person, the *agonisant*, to use the descriptive French term, writhing with pain, struggling in the throes of death. All traces of levity and wit quickly fade as Villon descends to the depths of the psyche where he rapidly and violently uncovers the ultimate pain, the ultimate horror, and perhaps most terrifying of all, the ultimate solitude of the human condition.

Here we have reached what may well be the darkest moment of the *Testament*. At this juncture Villon inserts a ballad which in its serenity and lyrical beauty contrasts sharply with the stark and violent imagery of the preceding stanza. This remarkable little piece, entitled by Clément Marot "Ballade des dames du temps jadis," has justly become one of the best known of all French poems.

Dictes moy ou, n'en quel pays,
Est Flora la belle Rommaine,
Archipiades ne Thaïs,
Qui fut sa cousine germaine,
Echo parlant quant bruyt on maine
Dessus riviere ou sus estan,
Qui beaulté ot trop qu'humaine.
Mais ou sont les neiges d'antan? (329-336)

(Tell me where, in what country
Is Flora the beautiful Roman
Archipiada or Thaïs
Who was first cousin to her once
Echo who speaks when there's a sound
Over pond or river
Whose beauty was more than human?
But where are the snows of last winter?).

The poem continues by citing other well known women, both fictional and historical personages, asking in every stanza where they are now. Although the *ubi sunt* theme occurs in the work of almost every major late medieval poet (notably Eustache Deschamps and Charles d'Orléans), Villon's ballad clearly detaches itself from other examples of the genre. This poem, with its crystalline clarity, its depth, its virtual artistic perfection, also far surpasses the other two *ubi sunt* ballads of Villon's trilogy, poems which, although no mediocre pieces, appear somewhat shallow by comparison.[4]

Even a superficial reading of the poem readily reveals an emphasis on the finite aspect of human existence, its highly perishable quality. But this piece is more than an eloquent lament on man's mortality, for this ballad, like the *Testament* itself, encloses within its embrace both life and death.[5] The question "Where are they now?" elicits two different answers. The first answer is that these women have vanished entirely. Yet, this explanation cannot be considered entirely satisfactory, for although their bodies, their physical beings have undoubtedly disappeared, their very names and the images associated with these names prove that some trace of their existence has been left behind. The second answer to the question, then, is that a part of their being remains, living on in the poem, constantly recreated and resurrected in the mind of each new reader.

Some of the women cited by Villon--Echo, Berte, Bietris, Alis, all characters from literature or mythology--never had any actual existence apart from the mind. As for the women who did once physically exist-- Flora, Heloïse, Joan of Arc, and the others--they have joined their fictional sisters in the realm of the imagination. The distinction between "real" and "imaginary" becomes effaced now that all the women are in effect imaginary. Both groups are allowed to coexist on an equal footing, the poet making no attempt to segregate or differentiate the two. Just as the historical characters of the ballad have been transformed from one dimension of existence to another, so Villon himself, in the very act of writing the *Testament*, is effecting the same transformation of his own existence, metamorphosizing the flesh-and-blood Villon into the paper-and-ink Villon with whom we have become (and continue to become) acquainted.

Continuity takes other forms in the poem. As each woman fades from view, she is replaced by another. The result is an unbroken chain of succession running throughout the ballad. If we let ourselves step back a bit from the poem, shifting our attention from the specific women who rapidly enter and exit to the succession itself, then we can see a certain pattern evolving. Transcending the limited duration of individual lives, womanhood endures. Feminine beauty, charm, mystique return with each new generation, proving equally potent in their capacity to seduce and influence men. To reduce the thought to its simplest terms: women and men die; Woman and Man do not.

Even at the level of poetic technique, the poem demonstrates a strong sense of coherence. The rich internal rhyme and melodic rhythm exemplified by the verse "Dessus riviere ou su estan" create a fluidity of movement maintained from beginning to end. The fact that all these stanzas as well as the *envoi* are framed within a question, or series of questions, contributes to the unity of tone and intonation. Finally, the very form of the ballad, with its inherent symmetry and the musical quality of its refrain, further reinforces the impression of continuity.

The last woman to appear in the poem is the Virgin Mary: "Ou sont ilz, ou, Vierge souvraine?" (351). Although all other women have disappeared, or will disappear, there is one who lives eternally, one who clearly embodies and immortalizes the highest qualities of womanhood, especially of motherhood. By ending with the figure of a mother, the most perfect and beloved of all mothers, Villon stresses the creative and nurturing aspect of femininity over the seductive and potentially destructive aspect exemplified by some of the women he has just cited. But the appearance of the Virgin implies something of still greater importance. Even as he poses the question to her, "Ou sont ilz...?", he is hinting at the nature of the answer he expects. The essential part of each woman, the core of her existence, that is to say her soul, is at this moment either with the Virgin, her spiritual mother, or hopelessly separated from her. Viewed in this religious context, the "Ou sont ilz..." ceases to be a rhetorical question, and becomes instead an urgent need to know the fate of something whose present existence cannot be subject to doubt. Villon's appeal to the Virgin adds a spiritual dimension to the poem, inviting a second reading with renewed attention to the poet's insistent question.

This repeated query takes two forms--one literal, one figurative--although both essentially pose the same question. Like the literal question, the figurative version, "Mais ou sont les neiges d'antan?", admits more than one answer. A factual response would simply state that the snows of the past have vanished. But in a poem so rich in meaning, such a patently logical conclusion seems flat and prosaic. A more poetic approach to the question, and one more in keeping with the symbolic character of the ballad, would take into account the cyclical continuity represented by the perpetual arrival and departure of winter's snow. So while the obvious answer to the question "Where are the women and the snows of the past?" is that they have dissolved and vanished without leaving a trace, another equally valid answer is that they constantly return, winter after winter, generation after generation. This is undeniably a poem about absence, loss, and death. It is also a poem about cycles, continuity, and renewal.

CHAPTER THREE: BARING BODY AND SOUL (Verses 413-532)

From the trilogy of ballads, each a variation of the *ubi sunt* theme, Villon moves into a consideration of time and its effect upon the human body and spirit. Rather than speaking in abstract terms or employing a variety of examples, he chooses to illustrate the degrading results of age by focusing attention on one particular person, a helmet-seller (the *Belle Heaulmière*, as she has come to be known), once noted for her beauty, now decrepit and pitiful. Villon imagines her soliloquy as she confronts with shock, disbelief, rage, and sorrow the ruin of her once beautiful body:

> Ha! vieillesse felonne et fiere,
> Pourquoi m'as si tost abatue?
> Qui me tient, qui, que ne me fiere,
> Et qu'a ce coup je ne me tue? (457-460)

> (Ah, cruel, arrogant old age
> Why have you beaten me down so soon?
> What holds me back from striking myself
> From killing myself with a blow?).

This woman, who has had the fortune to live a long life, complains not that she has become old, but that she has become old too soon. Here, as he does so often in the *Testament*, Villon exposes a weakness in human nature, in this case the difficulty, or even the impossibility, of gracefully accepting the aging process. The common tendency, exemplified by the reaction of the *Belle Heaulmière*, is to resist, deny, and protest the inevitable humiliations inflicted by old age. She perceives aging not as a natural and predictable phenomenon, a gradual passage from one stage of life to another, but rather as a cruel and brutal assault, unexpected and unwarranted. Yet in her state of utter despair, broken by her irresistible opponent and on the verge of suicide, she clings to what life she has, crying out in anger at the injustice she is forced to endure. In this attitude of simultaneous suffering and rebellion, in this painful and courageous confrontation of a hopeless dilemma, she momentarily overcomes her pathetic condition, and rises to nobility.

The *Belle Heaulmière* continues by lamenting the loss of her beauty and her seductive power over men. Rejecting the advances of numerous suitors, she reserved her love for a man who treated her contemptuously. As her plaint progresses, it becomes increasingly reminiscent of another unhappy voice we have recently heard. Her regret of misspent youth echos:

> Je plains le temps de ma jeunesse (169)

> (I mourn the days of my youth).

Her

> Que m'en reste il? Honte et pechié (484)

> (What's left? The shame and the sin)

calls to mind:

> Que toutes mes hontes j'euz beues (2)

> (When I had drunk down all my disgraces),

and

> Je suis pecheur, je le sçay bien (105)

> (I am a sinner I know it well).

Like the old woman, Villon consistently presents himself as victimized by time and men, isolated, wasted. The plight of the helmet-seller interests him not as a curious example of human degeneration, a mere digressionary movement in the flow of the poem, but as a powerful and moving drama with which he strongly identifies. The *Belle Heaulmière*, in fact, serves as a mask, thinly disguising the poet's presence. Throughout the *Testament* he will experiment with other masks while repeatedly acting out the same basic drama.

Contemplating her withered naked body, the *Belle Heaulmière* painfully confronts the physical evidence of time's passage:

> Quant je pense, lasse! au bon temps,
> Quelle fus, quelle devenue!
> Quant me regarde toute nue,
> Et je me voy si tres changiee,
> Povre, seiche, megre, menue,
> Je suis presque toute enragiee. (487-492)

(When I think alas of the happy times
What I was, what I've become
When I look at myself naked
And see how I've changed so much
Poor, dried-up, lean and bony
I nearly go off my head).

Her body silently but forcefully testifies to an act of extreme violence. Unlike the violence evidenced in Villon's graphic description of a dying person (313-328), the damage here has been inflicted gradually, painlessly, secretly. The results, nonetheless, are shocking in their devastation. With the memory of her youthful beauty cruelly vivid in her mind, the *Belle Heaulmière* faces the unpleasant reality of her present state. The emotional impact of the shattered illusion is cogently compressed into a single verse: "Quelle fus, quelle devenue." The mind's struggle to comprehend and accept the totally alien body to which it finds itself bound borders here on insanity, and the word *enraigee* should not be dismissed as mere hyperbole.

Proceeding now to inventory in painful detail the ravages of time upon her body, the old woman describes herself as she appears when stark naked. The tragic figure of the *Belle Heaulmière* surveying the remnants of her ruined physical charm foreshadows the stripped and humiliated Villon who will appear in various stages of nudity later in the poem:

J'en fus batu comme a ru telles,
Tout nu, ja ne le quier celer. (658-659)

(I was pummeled like laundry in a stream
Stark naked no need to hide it)

* * * * * *

Il fut rez, chief, barbe et sourcil,
Comme ung navet qu'on ret ou pelle. (1896-1897)

(They shaved his head, beard, and eyebrows
Like some turnip you scrape or peel).

* * * * * *

Tant que, d'icy a Roussillon,
Brosse n'y a ne brossillon
Qui n'eust, ce dit il sans mentir,
Ung lambeau de son cotillon.[1] (2007-2010)

(From here to Roussillon
There isn't a bush or shrub
That didn't get, he speaks truly
A shred from his back).

* * * * * *

Quant mourut n'avoit qu'ung haillon (2013)

(By the time he died he had only a rag).

Given the quantity of subtle and less subtle sexual innuendos present in this poem, one might reasonably expect any allusions to nakedness to be colored by a degree of carnality or lasciviousness, if not forthright obscenity, in short the *nuditas criminalis* flatly condemned by medieval theologians. The truth is, however, that only in one instance can a reference to nudity be taken as unequivocally provocative.[2] All other examples are aligned more closely to *nuditas virtualis*, the human anatomy representing purity and innocence rather than vanity and the desire for gratification.

Perhaps the most obvious significance of the poet's nakedness relates to the word *povre* which Villon repeatedly applies to himself.[3] In the exposed condition of the human body we are presented with a striking visual representation of the degrading effect of poverty. Nudity and poverty, it should be noted, were also linked on a linguistic level in the time of Villon, one of the meanings of *povre* being "stripped," one of the meanings of *poverté* being "private parts." The claim of poverty, together with allusions to various states of denudation and an admission of sinfulness are clearly intended to create a picture of humility, a picture we may or may not choose to take seriously.

Nakedness stands not only for poverty, but also for vulnerability. Associated with pain, punishment, and degradation, the unclothed figures of the *Testament* testify to the physical and moral frailty of human nature. The withered old woman, the stripped and beaten Villon, the bald, beardless, browless Villon, the dying rag-clad Villon, all have something to say about mortality. The late medieval fascination with death is also a fascination with the living body, its beauty, its weakness, its ever-changing character, its eventual decay. Each time in the poem we glimpse a naked figure, we are being invited to mock, lament, and contemplate the weakness of the flesh.

It is also the spiritual weakness of humanity that we witness in the exposed bodies of the *Testament*. The naked human form in medieval Christian art represents, among other things, a stigma of the original sin: "I heard thy voice in the garden, and I was afraid because I was naked."[4] Just as the poet's nakedness may be taken as the figurative equivalent of the declaration: "Povre je suis de ma jeunesse" (273), it may also be taken as the symbolic illustration of "Je suis pecheur, je le sçay bien" (105). Nakedness thus serves as a double reminder of human mortality, not only associated with physical vulnerability, but also recalling the origin of suffering and death according to Biblical tradition.

Not all the unclothed figures appearing in medieval religious art are necessarily reminiscent of the Fall. While Adam and Eve, the personifications of certain vices, and the damned souls of Hell are typically portrayed without clothing, the state of nudity is also associated with another important iconographic tradition--the Last Judgment. Here we see the dead, stripped of the trappings that distinguished their rank in life, rising out of their tombs to be judged.[5] The fact that Villon would choose to present himself and the *Belle Heaulmière* in the same attire they will wear on Judgment Day can hardly be considered coincidental, given the major role of the judgment theme in the *Testament*. The stripping away of clothing in the poem, it might be said, constitutes a rehearsal for the day when both body and soul will be laid bare, and all will be revealed.

The denuded figures of the poem, of course, need not be viewed exclusively from the perspective of religious symbolism. They may be taken equally well as images of the *Testament*'s humanistic quality, for in this poem we see humanity repeatedly stripped, figuratively and literally, of its disguises, its costumes, its layers of protective and decorative clothing, reduced ultimately to its essential nature. The result of this merciless divestitute with its attendant pain and disillusionment is a state of elemental purity. According to folkloric ritual, nakedness signifies a primordial state of existence associated with innocence and birth. This positive symbolic value may be partially attributed to the uncorrupted simplicity of the nude body. Nakedness may be seen as a negation, or at least an absence of some kind, as implied by the negative prefix of such words as "unclothed," "undressed," "uncovered." It is precisely the "un" character of this physical state that endows it with a sense of primitive innocence. What better form than that of a stripped man could be chosen then by a poet who consistently defines himself in terms of what he lacks?

Povre de sens et de savoir (178)

(Poor in sense and in knowledge)

* * * * * *

Qui n'ay ne cens, rente, n'avoir (180)

(Without cents, rent, or goods)

* * * * * *

Oncques de terre n'eust sillon (1888)

(He never owned a furrow of earth)

* * * * * *

Qui vaillant plat ne escuelle
N'eut oncques, n'ung brain de percil. (1894-1895)

(He didn't have the money for a plate or bowl
Or for a sprig of parsley).

Clearly, Villon does not flaunt the naked body with the intention of creating a vulgar spectacle. Whatever other symbolic implications may be attached to them, the stripped figures of the poem at the most basic level represent truth. Once the pretense of clothing is removed, one no longer appears as he wishes to be perceived, but as he truly is. The association of truth and nakedness can be found embedded even in our language: "the naked truth," or "la vérité toute nue." The bared bodies of the *Testament*, taken as tokens of truth, assure us that buried somewhere in this mischievously deceptive poem filled with irony, sarcasm, hyperbole, and double entendres, there are actually moments of sincerity, words that mean what they say, glimpses of naked truth. Paradoxically, the moments of greatest intimacy in this highly personal work are precisely those that speak most profoundly of the poem's universality. As the *povre Villon* and the *Belle Heaulmière* shed their clothes, reduced to a state of utter defenselessness, they lose their individual identities, becoming all men and all women at their weakest. It is when we see this old woman and this man who is no longer young stripped in every way, vulnerable, humiliated, suffering in despair, that we feel ourselves most to be their *frères humains*.

CHAPTER FOUR: The Procession of Martyred Lovers (Verses 533-672)

In the opening of the *Testament* Villon finds himself suspended in a state of limbo. Ultimately it is the confrontation with death that impels him to undertake a quest for the meaning of his existence, a quest which will continue, in one form or another, throughout the remainder of the poem. With the appearance of his alter ego the *Belle Heaulmière*, he symbolically strips himself of pretense and illusion in preparation for his journey of self-discovery. Now his spiritual quest continues. If the past offers no answers, only bitter memories, if death is not itself an answer but rather a looming question, and if the human condition is one of naked vulnerability, then what is one to do in this predicament? The *Belle Heaulmière* suggests one answer in the ballad addressed to female merchants in the prime of their youth:

> Or y pensez, belle Gantiere
> Qui m'escoliere souliez estre,
> Et vous, Blanche la Savetiere,
> Or est il temps de vous congnoistre.
> Prenez a destre et a senestre;
> N'espargnez homme, je vous prie. (533-538)

> (Now look here pretty Glover
> Who used to study under me
> And you too Blanche the Shoe-fitter
> It's time you got it straight
> Take what you can right and left
> Don't spare a man I beg you).

Her advice, simply stated, is to take all one can while capable of doing so. In one sense, her admonition appears highly cynical, an unscrupulous exhortation to pursue gratification at any price, even at the cost of human exploitation. On the other hand, one may also take her advice as a plea, grounded in wisdom and experience, to profit fully from the present moment, to actualize the immediate potential for happiness rather than defer self-fulfillment out of misplaced caution or prudence. Such advice, it may be argued, springs not from cynicism, but instead from a keen awareness of the uncertainty of life, its inherent risks and changeability. The helmet-seller compares the aging of women to the aging of coins:

> Car vielles n'ont ne cours ne estre.
> Ne que monnoye qu'on descrie. (539-540)

    (For there's no run on old crones
    No more than cried-down money).

Like monetary exchange, human commerce requires giving and taking, is not immune to exploitation, and requires repeated interaction to remain a dynamic process.

    Filled with sexual innuendos, the ballad recited by the ancient helmet-seller focuses attention, for the first time in the poem, on the sexual aspect of human relations. Villon has already touched lightly on the subject during the regretful recollections which open the *Testament*:

    Bien est verté que j'ay amé
    Et ameroie voulentiers;
    Mais triste cuer, ventre affamé
    Qui n'est rassasié au tiers
    M'oste des amoureux sentiers. (193-197)

    (It's true I have loved
    And willingly would love again
    But a heavy heart and starved crow
    Never full by more than a third
    Drag me down from love's ways).

The first two and a half verses are strongly reminiscent of the "classical" language of the traditional love lyric. The words *triste cuer* have a particularly courtly flavor, and prepare the reader for an introspective analysis of the lover's anguish. This expectation is thwarted, however, by the insertion of *ventre affamé* immediately after the cesura. The juxtaposition of heart and stomach deprives the former of its full metaphorical value, reminding us of its lesser status as another bodily organ. Once punctured, the courtly illusion rapidly deflates. Abstract language gives way to more colorful popular speech:

    Au fort, quelqu'ung s'en recompence,
    Qui est ramply sur les chantiers! (198-199)

    (By now someone else makes up the loss
    Who's filled to the brim in the gantry),

and finally evolves into the reworking of a proverbial phrase whose implication is anything but courtly:

Car la dance vient de la pance (200)

(For the dance starts in the belly).

Human love in the *Testament*, with one notable exception, is not the ethereal, uplifting force praised by the early French poets, the *trouvères* and the troubadours.[1] Brutally stripped of spiritual connotations, it is now reduced to a purely physical desire, a hunger as sharp and insistent as the hunger of the *ventre affamé*. Love, *Amors*, the lofty ideal of Villon's poetic predecessors, must be properly humbled before entering the world of the *Testament*.

The *Belle Heaulmière*, recognizing both the strength of carnal desire and the danger of denying its commands, recommends the manipulation of sexuality as a means of achieving material security and happiness. Anticipating a rebuttal of his view of love (for he implies that he shares the helmet-seller's sentiments), Villon states that his attitude does not result, as some might believe, from directing affection toward the wrong kind of women, women who are, either in fact or in effect, plain prostitutes. Love is corrupted, he maintains, not by the dishonorable character of a given woman, but by an inherent flaw of human nature. As evidence of the destructive power of love, he has already cited the cases of Abelard and Buridan in the "Ballade des dames du temps jadis" (337-43). But the greatest concentration of love's victims is found in the "Double Ballade" which now follows the poet's prefatory remarks on the nature of love.[2] An admonition to would-be lovers opens the poem:

> Pour ce, amez tant que vouldrez,
> Suyvez assemblees et festes,
> En la fin ja mieulx n'en vauldrez
> Et n'y romprez que vos testes. (625-628)

> (So fall in love all you want
> Go to dances and festivals
> Come home empty-handed
> With nothing cracked but your skulls).

The last two verses announce a series of images connecting love with acts of violence and violation. The "cracking" of heads is meant to be taken figuratively as well as literally. Love promises either the collapse of reason or a broken skull. In either case it will always bring out man's bestial nature. "Car la dance vient de la pance." And now the degrading dance begins:

Salmon en ydolatria,
Samson en perdit ses lunetes. (630-631)

(It made an idolater of Solomon
And that's why Samson lost his eyes).

Here Villon juxtaposes two acts of violation: the transgression of divine commandment in the first instance, of nature itself in the second. The blinding is physical in one case, spiritual in the other. Solomon's idolotry illustrates the power of love to disorient minds, corrupt moral judgment, "crack heads." The mutilation inflicted upon Samson, like the castration of Abelard, represents the crippling power of love, whether it is conscience, virility, or vision that is damaged.

Shifting from Biblical to Classical tradition, Villon introduces the figures of Orpheus and Narcissus into the procession:

Orpheüs, le doux menestrier,
Jouant de fleustes et musetes,
En fut en dangier d'un murtrier
Chien Cerberus a quatre testes. (633-636)

(Love made the sweet minstrel Orpheus
Playing his flutes and bagpipes
Risk death from the murderous
Dog four-headed Cerberus).

Orpheus, like Buridan, only achieves the status of a potential martyr. Although unsuccessful in his attempt to rescue Eurydice from the underworld, he never suffers bodily injury from the dangers of Hades. The "descent" of Narcissus forms a skillfully constructed parallel:

Et Narcisus, le bel honnestes,
En ung parfont puis s'en noya
Pour l'amour de ses amouretes. (637-639)

(It made the fair-haired boy Narcissus
Drown himself down in a well
For love of his lovelies).

Orpheus and Narcissus both voluntarily enter the realm of death in search of a loved one. Both are unsuccessful. The former is allowed to return to life, while the latter, having pursued an illusion, is not.

Following Narcissus comes Sardana (an abbreviated form of Sardana-
pale, the legendary king of Assyria):

> Sardana, le preux chevalier,
> Qui conquist le regne de Cretes,
> En voulut devenir moullier
> Et filler entre pucelletes. (641-644)

> (It made the brave knight Sardana
> Who subdued the whole kingdom of Crete
> Try to turn into a woman
> So he could join the virgins at spinning).

The most obvious function of Sardana is to provide another example of
reason lost to love. There is, however, another loss subtly implied in these
verses. The *preux* Sardana, willing to give up his *prouesse*, the very quality
which guarantees his manhood, "voulut devenir mouillier." The use of the
simple past tense indicates an attempted act rather than an unfulfilled wish.
The notion of a soldier trying to become a woman brings to mind the fate of
the poor Abelard.

Next comes another series of Biblical allusions, beginning with
David's illicit love for Bathsheba:

> David le roy, sage prophetes,
> Crainte de Dieu en oublia,
> Voyant laver cuisses bien faites. (645-647)

> (And made King David the wise prophet
> Forget all fear of God
> When he saw shapely thighs being washed).

The Hebrew king, attracted by the beauty of Bathsheba, promptly had her
husband Uriah sent to the battlefront. The strategy worked perfectly: Uriah
died a hero's death, leaving his wife conveniently widowed. In carrying out
his plan, however, David overlooked a number of commandments, and thus
incurred divine displeasure. With his usual ellipsis, Villon condenses the
story into three verses. Again violence and violation are paired, and
although his name is unmentioned, there is another victim.

The Biblical episode that follows contains a greater degree of
perversion:

> Amon en voult dehonnourer,
> Faignant de menger tarteletes,
> Sa seur Thamar et desflourer,
> Qui fut inceste deshonnestes. (649-652)

> (It made Amnon want to dishonor
> While pretending to be eating tarts
> His sister Tamar and deflower her
> Which was wicked incest).

Tamar, the only female victim of the "Double Ballade," is the object of both moral and physical violation in the dual crime of incest and rape. The story does not end here. Absolom, brother of Tamar and half brother of Amnon, waited patiently for the moment of vengeance to arrive. When Amnon eventually let himself be lured into a helpless state of drunkenness, he was slain by Absolom's servants. Love, as we are shown, whether incestuous, self-centered, or adulterous, always produces the same results.

Closing the trilogy of Biblical allusions is the death of John the Baptist whom Herod ordered decapitated:

> Pour dances, saulx et chansonnetes (655)

> (For dances, leaps, and love songs).

At this point Villon introduces himself into the cast of legendary characters:

> De moy, povre, je vueil parler:
> J'en fus batu comme a ru telles,
> Tout nu, ja ne le quier celer. (657-659)

> (Of my poor self let me say
> I was pummeled like laundry in a stream
> Stark naked no need to hide it).

He blames his beating on a certain Katherine de Vausselles, who may have been his mistress. The word *povre* in the first verse is both a remark of self-pity and an apology for including within the ranks of such illustrious figures so humble a personage as the *povre Villon*. The flogging inflicted upon Villon's naked body may allude, as some have speculated, to an act of corporal punishment for some crime, possibly adultery. Villon's appearance at the end of the procession is clearly calculated to inspire humor as much as commiseration. Behind the looming figures of myth and antiquity, magnified by their cruelty or their suffering, follows the poor little Villon, utterly naked, cursing and muttering threats under his breath. Yet in spite of the scene's strong comic overtones, a tragic element is also present, for Villon (if we are to judge by all he tells us of his experience with love) deserves a place among the ranks of love's victims. The figure of the humbled poet bringing up the rear of the procession reintroduces a personal note into the *Testament*, the poem never being allowed to deviate long from its introspective orientation.

One avenue of escape from the human condition of isolation has proven only to lead back to misery. Love, the attraction that draws together man and woman, the powerful emotional force that could offer some measure of joy and consolation, generally becomes corrupted, according to Villon's view, by the human tendency to abuse and destroy that which should be held precious. As for the *Belle Heaulmière*'s words of advice, they merely point to a temporary solution, failing to address the underlying malaise of the human condition. Villon will need to look elsewhere for the answer.

CHAPTER FIVE: A MOTHER'S PRAYER (Verses 865-909)

The "Double Ballade" is followed by a bitter denunciation and renunciation of Love who Villon claims has treated him very badly indeed. Returning to the fiction of the will after some eight hundred verses of preliminary remarks, the poet finally begins the formal dictation of his testament. The poem momentarily takes on a documentary character as standard religious and legalistic formulas are interspersed within the text.[1] The dying narrator of the *Testament* wills his soul to *Nostre Dame*, his body to the earth, "nostre grant mere la terre" (842), his library to Guillaume de Villon, his adoptive father. Next he turns to his mother. To her he leaves a special gift, a prayer she may offer to the Virgin Mary:

> Dame du ciel, regente terrienne,
> Emperiere des infernaux palus,
> Recevez moy, vostre humble chrestienne,
> Que comprinse soye entre vos esleus. (873-876)

> (Lady of heaven, regent of earth
> Empress over the swamps of hell
> Receive me your humble Christian
> Let me be counted among your elect).

This poetic prayer, eloquent in its candor and simplicity, so solemn and humble in tone, gives a new turn to the *Testament*.[2] The elusive poem which has alternately taken the form of a personal memoir, a philosophical meditation, most recently a scathing diatribe, now becomes a kind of hymn. The simplicity of expression may be explained by the ignorance of the speaker, a woman whose religious instruction is virtually limited to what she sees painted on the walls of her parish church:

> Au moustier voy dont suis paroissienne
> Paradis paint, ou sont harpes et lus,
> Et ung enfer ou dampnez sont boullus. (895-897)

> (On the walls of my parish church I see
> A paradise painted with harps and lutes
> And a hell where they boil the damned).

Villon's mother acknowledges herself as a sinner unworthy of the Virgin's goodness, then humbly begs that Mary intercede on her behalf. The poem ends with a profession of faith containing Villon's name in acrostic:

Vous portastes, digne Vierge, princesse,
Iesus regnant qui n'a ne fin ne cesse.
Le Tout Puissant, prenant nostre foiblesse,
Laissa les cieulx et nous vint secourir,
Offrit a mort sa tres chiere jeunesse;
Nostre Seigneur tel est, tel le confesse:
En ceste foy je vueil vivre et mourir. (903-909)

(Virgin so worthy, princess, you bore
Iesus who reigns without end or limit
Lord Almighty who took on our weakness
Left heaven and came down to save us
Offering his precious youth to death
Now such is our Lord, such I acknowledge him
In this faith I want to live and die).

Since acrostics are not uncommon in the fifteenth century, this particular example could be taken as a purely gratuitous act, the signature of the artist identifying a work as his own. Villon's poetry, however, unlike the verse of his contemporaries, consistently avoids gratuity and superficiality, and we may be sure that the VILLON of the *envoi* constitutes more than just an innocuous appendage to the poem. To use the metaphor of a painting, we should not view the artist's name as appearing in the lower margin of the canvas, excluded from the picture proper, but rather as lying within and inseparable from the painting itself.[3]

The transparency of the poem's idiom easily lulls the reader into accepting the ballad at face value, and as long as we listen to the poem as a recitation, it appears perfectly straightforward. When we look at the closing stanza as a visual image, however, the text becomes more complicated. One's first impulse is to isolate the acrostic from the *envoi* in order to set it more sharply in relief. Viewed next as an integral part of the stanza, the acrostic naturally drifts back into the body of the poem, and another pattern becomes visible:

Vous
Iesus
Le Tout Puissant
Laissa
Offrit
Nostre Seigneur

The acrostic VILLON is formed largely from words designating a sacred presence. What, if anything, is the meaning of this curious association? One fact which soon becomes apparent is that the poet has literally based his name on his verse. The name of Villon is in effect doubly immortalized, linked not only to the poem which will outlive the man, but also to the eternal concepts embodied in the words "Jesus," "Le Tout Puissant," "Nostre Seigneur." Continuing to explore the symbolic dimensions of this verbal association, we discover that the three sacred names whose first letter is contained in the acrostic represent the three persons of the Trinity: "Jesus regnant qui n'a ne fin ne cesse" (Holy Spirit), "Le Tout Puissant" (Father), "Nostre Seigneur" (Son). If the name VILLON takes its form, its being in part from the Trinity, then could it follow that Villon, the man, grounds his existence on the same? Here is the riddle hidden in the name hidden in the poem. Once the question has been raised, there exists the possibility, if not the temptation, of reading the acrostic as a symbolic parallel to the direct articulation of the mother's credo.

With the acrostic Villon is inviting us, indeed challenging us to read his poetry, figuratively and literally, from different angles. For example:

V
I
L
L
O
N
En ceste foy je vueil vivre et mourir.

The visual image of the poet's name still fresh in our minds, we reread the refrain and find that the *je* has assimilated a second identity. Villon, who has momentarily effaced his presence, allowing his mother to recite her soliloquy, now steps forward to join her in the culmination of her prayer. His appearance is not totally unannounced. His mother is characterized as *povrecte* and *pecheresse*, descriptions he has already applied to himself.[4] Another forewarning of Villon's entry into the poem comes in the stanza prefacing the ballad. The mention of *nostre Maistresse* (866) leads Villon to consider his relationship to the Virgin:

Autre chastel n'ay, ne fortresse,
Ou me retraye corps et ame,
Quant sur moy court malle destresse,
Ne ma mere, la povre femme! (869-872)

(I've no other castle or fortress
Where I can find refuge body and soul
When evil times come upon me
And my mother hasn't either, poor woman).[5]

The stanza is dominated not by the nature of the legacy or by the relationship between Villon's mother and the Virgin, but rather by the poet's attitude toward his earthly and especially toward his heavenly mother. It is on this deeply personal note that he moves into the "Ballade pour prier Nostre Dame." One function of the acrostic is to remind the reader that although the poet is expressing himself through the intermediary of his mother, it is, factually speaking, Villon, the composer of the poem/prayer, who is addressing the Virgin. More than a gift, the ballad is an offering, and one must remain mindful of its ultimate source as well as its final destination.

Given the medieval respect for the evocative power of the written word, Villon's acrostic signature may convey yet another meaning. By transferring his being into a written name, Villon symbolically incorporates himself into the text of the prayer, thus assuring his ascension (at least in name) with the ascension of his mother's prayer. Like a clever stowaway, he conceals himself within his mother's words, and lets himself be taken before his *Maistresse.* By carrying the name of Villon in her prayer, the poet's mother is actually praying not only for her own salvation, but also, as one mother to another, for the salvation of her son.

The letters VILLON must ultimately be taken as a message, a sign, to use the structuralist term. By their vertical arrangement on the page, they dissociate themselves from the linear progression of the stanza, and fall within another plane of interpretation. Once the poet's name has been uncovered, it would seem that the message has been decoded. But close scrutiny of one hidden message reveals the possible existence of another. Either Villon is merely labeling the poem as his own (as the *trouvères* occasionally identify themselves in the closing lines of the *envoi*), in which case the acrostic is little more than a neat sleight of hand, or he is making a symbolic statement that deserves our closest attention.

On the other hand, it must be recognized that whatever importance may be attached to Villon's acrostic signature, the poet is careful to disguise his appearance in the poem, and any symbolic statement he may be making is therefore tentative at this point. The acrostics "FRANÇOYS" and "VILLON" will appear later in the *Testament*, embedded in poems whose tone is quite different from the "Ballade pour prier Nostre Dame."[6] This apparent contradiction only reinforces the paradoxical nature of the *Testament*, its lack of predictability, its baffling inconsistencies, all of which contribute to its personal character.

CHAPTER SIX: THE LEGACIES (Verses 910-1835)

With the bequeathal of his library to Guillaume de Villon, and the ballad left to his mother, Villon opens a long series of legacies comprised of more than fifty separate bequests, and covering almost one thousand verses. This section of the *Testament*, filled with names and places commonplace to Parisian citizens in 1461 but completely foreign to modern readers, is undoubtedly the most difficult portion of the poem. Thanks to the research of numerous scholars, the majority of the people and sites mentioned by Villon have now been identified. Still, a considerable number of passages alluding to specific incidents in the poet's past have yet to be satisfactorily explained. The novice reader of the *Testament* would be well advised to move slowly through this section of the text with a good commentary in hand, patiently and methodically identifying unfamiliar names.[1] This bit of detective work, although possibly appearing tedious at first, will soon reward the diligent reader with a minimal acquaintance with Villon's Paris, a knowledge that will greatly enhance his reading of the poem.

One of the most striking aspects of the legacies is the emotional and intellectual energy they convey. Anger, violence, humor, sexuality are all to be found in abundance here, giving this part of the poem a remarkable sense of vitality. While the first section of the *Testament* shows some evidence of restraint and moderation, the legacies open a floodgate of emotion. As the poet passes from one legatee to another, pausing rarely for reflection, he attains and manages to sustain a rapid, almost frantic pace.

Rather than attempt a verse-by-verse analysis of this lengthy passage, a monumental task which in any case would duplicate existing commentaries, this chapter will focus on the salient features of the legacies and the broad patterns they form when taken as a whole. Several of the ballads included among the bequests will be considered separately in a subsequent chapter.

The Heirs

The people named as recipients of Villon's gifts fall into five general categories. First there are the poet's personal acquaintances: his mother and Guillaume de Villon; Marthe, his former mistress; Jehan Cotart, his lawyer; Noel Jolis, a companion. Perhaps Jacques Raguier, son of a royal cook and a young man with quite a reputation as a drinker, and two prostitutes identified only as Marion and Jehanne can also be placed in this category. It is likely that Villon knew them, but we cannot be certain. The legatees with whom Villon was personally acquainted, members of his own social class whose company he must have shared on a regular basis, are actually relatively few in number.

The largest group of heirs is comprised of prominent Parisian citizens, mostly wealthy bourgeois whom Villon treats with contempt: Pierre Merebeuf, Nicolas de Louvier, and Jacquet Cardon, all prosperous merchants; Jehan and François Perdrier, sons of a rich money-changer; Andry Courault, a distinguished attorney; Madamoiselle de Bruyère, the owner of a well-known inn. By and large these are people with whom Villon must have had very little if any contact. The disdain which they inspire probably results more than the poet's attitude toward the social class they represent than from a desire for revenge.

Such is not the case for the third category of legatees, the municipal officials and officers of the law with whom Villon, the criminal, had experienced so many difficulties: the *unze vingts sergens*, the municipal police; Macé d'Orléans, a judge; Jehan Laurens, the prosecutor who handled the theft of Navarre; Jehan Cornu, Perrenet, Basanier, and others who staffed the infamous prison of the Châtelet.

Members of the clergy also number among Villon's "beneficiaries": the mendicant friars; brother Baude, a Carmelite friar; Guillaume Cotin and Thibaut de Vitry, elderly canons of Notre Dame; maistre Lomer, an ecclesiastic also connected with the same cathedral. The last group of legatees might be termed the *misérables*, the traditional recipients of charity whom one would expect to find named in a will: the patients of the *Ostel Dieu*, a large hospital; the *enffans trouvés*, orphans housed in a municipal orphanage; the *quinze-vingts*, inmates in a home for the blind.

The richness of Villon's poem lies not only in its bewildering variety of styles and tones, but also in the breadth of humanity it embraces. Just as the *danse macabre* indiscriminately unites figures representing every stratum of society, Villon's will encompasses men and women of every social and moral condition. Here we find side by side judges, clergymen, and prostitutes, shady characters and upstanding citizens, the wealthiest and the most destitute residents of Paris. Stripped of the distinctions that set them apart outside the poem, all are equalized upon entering the private world of the *Testament*. Now that wealth, prestige, and power have been rendered useless, the men who once hid behind these defenses become completely vulnerable.

Villon, once the helpless victim, is now omnipotent. It is he who controls those who have always controlled him. Their fates rest precariously in his hands. Through his equivocal gifts Villon gives out sexual potency, the right to be loved, an indulgence, a beating, and a hangman's noose, as his humor moves him. He deprives a judge of his virility, turning him into a woman, and transforms three wealthy usurers into penniless orphans. The legacies, however, are rarely random acts of malice, but stem rather from a strong sense of justice. Villon, no longer the accused, now assumes the role of the judge, handing out the sentences that in his estimation each "defendant" deserves. If a particular judgment strikes us as unduly harsh, we may be sure that some keenly felt injury underlies the severity of the punishment.

The writing of a will has, among other functions, the purpose of settling one's affairs, putting them in final order while one still has the capacity to do so. The section of legacies in the *Testament*, as chaotic as it may appear, rests on certain principles of unity and order, one of which is the redress of past wrongs. The normal order of society with its rigid and inequitable system of justice has been replaced by a personal sense of moral order that rejects smugness, hypocrisy, and false superiority. Underlying the coarse and insulting punishments meted out to Villon's victims is not only a natural desire for revenge, but also an acute sensitivity to injustice. The legacies represent a methodic attempt to bring some element of order into the emotional turmoil evident throughout the poem.

In the legacy section, the *Testament* takes on a certain farcical quality as the poet transforms old men into children, changes men of disreputable character into paragons of virtue, endows the impotent with potency. Once the reader becomes familiar with Villon's technique of antiphrasis, the use of words to designate the opposite of what they normally signify, he naturally tends to focus more on what the poet implies than what he actually says. Our reading of the legacies may be enriched, however, if we momentarily disregard the hidden implications of Villon's bequests, and simply study the surface of the text. When taken together, the transformations that Villon puts into effect form a pattern of redemption. Prostitutes become respectable women, corrupt merchants become destitute orphans, sadistic jailers become good and honest men. Just as the legacies redress the wrongs Villon has personally experienced, they also, at another level, restore an element of purity and innocence to a corrupt society. It may be argued that throughout the legacy section Villon's primary intention is to devastate his enemies with the weapon of sarcasm he wields so admirably. This premise can hardly be refuted. The "rehabilitation" of the legatees is clearly meant to be ironic. Nonetheless, in the process of disguising their identity, Villon is reminding us, whether deliberately or inadvertently, that greedy old men were once carefree boys, prostitutes were once honorable women, and corrupt police agents have at least a capacity for goodness and honesty. The restitution of innocence, even when carried out for the purpose of mockery, represents in itself a kind of gift. Villon, uncharitable though he may be, becomes in more than one sense the benefactor of his beneficiaries.

The Bequests

Almost every gift listed in the *Testament* is equivocal. The bequest to Guillaume Charruau, about whom practically nothing is known, typifies the ambiguous nature of the legacies:

> Item, donne a mon advocat,
> Maistre Guillaume Charruau,
> Quoy? qu'il marchande ou ait estat,
> Mon branc; je me tais du fourreau.
> Il aura avec ung rëau
> En change, affin que sa bource enfle. (1022-1027)

> (*Item* I give to my lawyer
> Master Guillaume Charruau
> My cutlass but not the sheath
> Never mind that Marchant got it first
> To swell out his purse I also give
> A *reau* in small change).[2]

Given that *branc* signifies "excrement" as well as "cutlass," and that *reau*, a gold coin, is a homonym of *rot*, "burp," it is clear that Villon's donation to Charruau is somewhat less generous than it first appears. In the same manner Villon, the verbal magician, turns a felt band into a hangman's noose, a cheese pie into a slap, copper coins into scabs. Offering something desirable only to slyly substitute something highly undesirable or even offensive, Villon repeatedly carries out his practical jokes. The playful nature of these equivocal legacies effectively turns the poem into a game; Villon tells us what he is supposedly leaving to a given legatee, and the reader must discover what he is actually giving in disguise. The contrast between the stated and implied legacies, the metamorphosis which many of the legatees are forced to undergo, as well as the feigned concern the dying writer of the will shows for his beneficiaries, all provide a rich source of humor. Full of irony, mockery, and flippancy, the legacies supply a lengthy diversion from the subjects of suffering, sin, and death that play so prominent a role in the early part of the *Testament.*

It would seem that Villon has temporarily abandoned the philosophical issues he raised earlier in the poem. Still, something important is taking place in the legacy section. Through the levity, frivolity, and obscenity of the legacies, Villon is drawing our attention to the role of illusion in the poem. The *Testament*, after all, is the fictitious will of a man who, pretending to be dying, leaves equivocal or even non-existent gifts to people whose true identity has often been disguised. Even the master deceiver admits that he himself has been the victim of deceit. Speaking of an unnamed mistress, Villon recalls how easily she misled him:

> Abusé m'a et fait entendre
> Tousjours d'ung que se fust ung aultre,
> De farine que ce fust cendre,
> D'ung mortier ung chappeau de faultre,
> De viel machefer que fust peaultre. (689-693)

> (I was so turned around I believed
> Always one thing was another
> That wheat flour was potash
> And a mortar a felt hat
> That old furnace slag was pewter).

The primary tool of deceit, of course, is language, and Villon teaches us through his legacies to approach his words cautiously and suspiciously. If he calls a man young and handsome, it is almost certain that he is old and ugly. If he calls another generous, we may reasonably assume that he is

miserly. The danger is that the reader, believing he has finally caught on to
the game, will take every verse of the poem to be necessarily equivocal. If
this assumption were correct, the *Testament* would become a simpler, more
predictable, less interesting poem that it actually is.

In the process of distributing gifts, Villon assumes a variety of roles.
At one point he claims the status of a doctor:

> J'ordonne, moy qui suis son miege (1140)

> (As his doctor I order him).

Sometimes he is a highly placed official of the Church freely granting
ecclesiastical privileges. At other moments he becomes a civil official. Not
content with these positions of authority, Villon appropriates supernatural
powers:

> Item donne a maistre Lomer,
> Comme extraict que je suis de fee,
> Qu'il soit bien amé..... (1796-1798)

> (*Item* I leave to master Lomer
> The gift of being well loved
> Which I can give by my fairy blood).

He also makes use of his superhuman abilities by joining together two hills,
Montmartre and mount Valerian, a hill to the west of Paris. In the act of
giving, Villon realizes a high degree of sustained vitality and creativity. It is
at this point in the *Testament* that he fully assumes his powers as creator of
the imaginary world over which he has omnipotent control.

In the fiction of the *Testament* the *povre Villon* gives away all he has.
Similarly, the poet Villon, throughout the poem but especially in the legacy
section, gives much of himself--his humor and anger, his delight and
bitterness, his memories, his poetry. Drawn from an abundance of emotion
and inspiration, the legacies convey an extraordinary sense of plenitude and
energy. The *povre Villon*, as we discover, is a man of remarkable wealth.

Sexuality

If for nothing else, the *Testament* is widely known for its obscenity, its sexual allusions, the scabrous aspect of its character. Villon's barbs frequently take the form of sexual insults, implying impotence and questioning virility. There is, paradoxically, a constructive as well as a destructive pattern to Villon's sexual allusions. Lost desire, for example, is systematically replaced by sexual potency. Claiming that he is no longer attracted to his mistress, Villon relinquishes her to those who can respond as he cannot:

> Mes plus grand dueilz en sont passez,
> Plus n'en ay le croppion chault.
> Si m'en desmetz aux hoirs Michault,
> Qui fut nommé le Bon Fouterre. (920-923)

> (My worst griefs have all gone by
> And I no longer get it up
> I stand aside for the heirs of Michault
> Who was known as "The Great Fucker").

Playing with tavern signs, the poet identifies Pierre Saint Amant, the Clerk of the Treasury, with *le Cheval Blanc*, and his wife with *la Mulle*, then continues the game by pairing the horse and the mule with more vivacious mates:

> Pour *le Cheval Blanc* qui ne bouge
> Luy chanjay a une jument
> Et *la Mulle* a ung asne rouge. (1011-1013)

> ("The White Horse" who can't move
> I mate instead with a mare
> And "The She-Mule" with a red-hot ass).

Villon's gifts repeatedly attempt to kindle carnal desire. To two wealthy bourgeois he grants a sexual adventure. He urges servants and chambermaids to enjoy each other's company after their masters have retired for the evening. As a remedy to the frustration of the *filles de bien* ("nice girls") he suggests they turn to equally frustrated monks:

> Si fussent ilz de peu contentes:
> Grant bien leur fissent mains loppins
> Aux povres filles (ennementes!)
> Qui se perdent aux Jacoppins. (1571-1574)

(If only they could made do with little
How nice for the poor girls
To get certain large morsels
Now wasting away with the Jacobins).

To Jehan Mahé, a guard at the Châtelet, Villon leaves a hundred cloves of Saracen ginger, a potent aphrodisiac according to medieval superstition:

Non pas pour acouppler ses boetes,
Mais pour conjoindre culz et coetes,
Et couldre jambons et andoulles. (1121-1123)

(Not for nailing his boxes
But for joining cunts and cocks
And attaching hams to sausages).

One result of Villon's legacies is obviously to evoke humor, usually at someone else's expense. Another result, not so readily apparent, is to restore a free and healthy sexuality where one is lacking. The society that Villon creates on the surface of the legacies is one of young, attractive, innocent people of high moral character. It is also a society in which the free expression of sexuality is sanctioned, and even encouraged. It is, in short, a utopia which, like any utopia, has only one flaw--it is completely imaginary.

On the other hand, the whole of the *Testament* insofar as it represents the will of a dying man is fictitious, and the fact that Villon's "utopia" does not correspond to the reality of fifteenth-century Parisian society need not preclude this element of fantasy from any serious consideration. A sensitive reading of the *Testament*, of any poem in fact, must go beyond the sifting of reality from fantasy with the intention of discarding the latter. Nothing can be neglected. If the poet chooses to conceal his primary meaning in images that serve as a camouflage, then the patterns generated by these images also deserve attention. In the case of the *Testament*, it has been shown that the legacies when read superficially yield an idyllic picture of society. Equally significant, it is a picture from which the poet, as creator, is virtually excluded.

Violence

If Villon as a dramatic character is absent from the legacies, his poetic presence can be felt everywhere. The dying old man calmly and generously parcelling out his possessions among his friends only thinly disguises the cunning young man capable of vicious verbal assaults on his enemies. Through the long series of legacies runs a thread of violence. To Jehan Raguier, one of the mounted sergeants who formed the personal guard of the Provost of Paris, Villon makes a seemingly innocuous bequest:

> Tant qu'il vivra, ansi l'ordonne,
> Tous les jours une tallemouse. (1072-1073)

> (A cream puff a day
> For the rest of his life, I order it).

The little gift becomes less innocent once we realize that *tallemouse* also designates a blow in the face. We can only wonder what Raguier can have done to deserve such a punishment. Françoys de la Vacquerie, the bishop's attorney charged with prosecuting cases involving clerics, a man whom Villon obviously had reason to detest, is the recipient of a *gorgerin d'Escossoys* (1216), a Scottish gorget but also a noose. A similar gift is made to the municipal police:

> A chascun une grant cornete
> Pour pendre a leurs chappeaulx de faultres. (1090-1091)

> (I give them each a stout chinstrap[3]
> For dangling from their felt hats).

One can easily surmise the other meaning of *cornete*, a meaning which throws a different light on the verb *pendre* in the following verse. To the *Scelleur* (Keeper of the Seal) Villon thoughtfully leaves a *poulce escachie* (1202), a "thumb crushed flat," presumably to facilitate the application of wax seals. Noel Jolis, whom Villon holds responsible for the failure of an unidentified escapade, receives two hundred and twenty lashes. Colin Galerne, a barber who somehow managed to antagonize Villon, is left a block of ice from the Marne with orders to keep it firmly pressed against his stomach all winter. If he complies with this request, Villon assures him, he need not worry about feeling too warm the following summer.

Other legacies, while not overtly violent or injurious, display a
definite streak of cruelty. To the people living in the *Ostel Dieu* and in the
poorhouses of Paris, the most wretched and unfortunate of Villon's fellow
citizens, the poet, claiming first that any joking would be out of place here,
leaves nothing but goose bones. To the blind of Paris, who could hardly
have done him any wrong, he leaves his eyeglasses to use in the Cemetery of
the Innocents where they beg alms:

> Pour mettre a part, aux Innocens,
> Les gens de bien des deshonnestes. (1734-1735)
>
> (For telling apart at the Innocents
> The rich folks from the crooked).

In Villon's defense it should be observed that gratuitous cruelty of this
sort is rare in the *Testament*. Most of the "negative" gifts are either playful
jabs at well-known figures, or retributions for personal offenses. The
sadistic bequests to the poor and the blind do, however, point to the dark
side of the *Testament*. As a journey into the depths of the psyche, the poem
reveals the human capacity for malice as well as for goodness. A medieval
theologian would have little difficulty extracting evidence of the seven
deadly sins from this poem. The most serious of these, the sin of pride,
asserts itself tenaciously throughout the legacy section where Villon,
placing himself in the role of the judge, elevates himself to a position of
moral superiority over those whom he condemns to humiliation.

Money

Not all of Villon's bequests are completely unconventional. A number
of the legacies are of a financial nature, covering a variety of monetary
denominations: *escu, targe, reau, angelot, ange, sou*. To one legatee he
bequeathes four handfuls of money; to a couple of wealthy old canons he
gives ecclesiastical stipends. There is nothing patently unusual about the
role of money in the *Testament*, a poem which, after all, claims to be a will.
In any case, by the fifteenth century, virtually every literary genre had been
invaded by financial terminology, a phenomenon that may be partially
explained by the steadily increasing influence of the bourgeois class. Even
the lexicon of the courtly lyric, formerly immune to such linguistic
incursions, was showing evidence of commercial "contamination."

Money in the *Testament* is an illusory commodity. First, since Villon constantly protests his absolute poverty, he obviously has no financial estate to divide among his heirs. But the majority of all Villon's bequests, including the non-financial gifts, are pure fabrications, and cannot be dismissed simply because they belong to the fictitious aspect of the poem. Villon's money, when studied closely, proves to be an interesting type of counterfeit. The *escu* and the *targe* (917) turn out to be male genitals. The *reau* (1026) is actually a burp. Four *placques* (1040) are nothing but scabs, and two *angelotz* (1272) are really cheeses. By systematically "devaluing" the currency of his day, Villon is implicitly questioning the value of material wealth. At one point he achieves the same effect by raising the value of money, mixing religious and monetary language:

Ave salus, tiby decus.[4] (1287)

The *salut* and the *ecu*, two common coins, are endowed here with quasi-sacred status. This parody should not be taken as a mockery of the religious sentiment embodied in the Latin hymn to the Virgin, but rather as a commentary on the respect and even reverence that money has come to command.

Coins, like words, are essentially symbols, and Villon enjoys playing with the symbolic value of both. But there is a serious side to this game. By contrasting the abstraction of money with concrete reminders of basic human needs, Villon emphasizes the artificiality of financial exchange, and, at a deeper level, questions the accumulation of monetary wealth as an end in itself.

Wine

Although they do not necessarily play a dominant role in the legacies, frequent references to wine, taverns and drinking are to be found scattered throughout this section of the poem. Two illustrious drinkers are cited: Jacques Raguier and Jehan Cotart, and the latter's fondness for drink is eulogized in a facetious prayer. Villon leaves fourteen hogsheads of wine to one heir, recommends to valets and chambermaids that they consume six or

seven pints as a prelude to their nocturnal activities, promises to pay Robert
Turgis, a tavern owner, for all the wine he has consumed (provided that
Robert can find him). Two taverns, *le Grand Godet* ("The Big Wine Cup")
and *le Barillet* ("The Wine Keg") are given as gifts (1039, 1359). In the
"Ballade de la Grosse Margot" we see Villon again distributing the popular
beverage:

> Quant viennent gens, je cours et happe ung pot,
> Au vin m'en fuis, sans demener grant bruit (1595-1596))

> (When clients come I run and get a cup
> And go for wine taking care to be quiet).

The tavern is obviously a milieu with which Villon is well acquainted,
and the *Testament* in some respects--given its occasional coarseness, its
obscenities, and salty language--is a kind of tavern song. Furthermore, the
legacies, leaping wildly about in a sequence whose true logic can only exist
in the poet's mind, may be fairly characterized as (figuratively speaking) the
product of an intoxicated imagination. Leaving far behind the sobering
spiritual questions that haunt the opening of the poem, Villon now
introduces a Dionysian element into the *Testament*, temporarily eluding
death with gaiety, jesting, and mockery. Just as he generously distributes
wine in his legacies, Villon also freely dispenses a verbal intoxicant which
keeps the reader, more than slightly disoriented by now, from dwelling on
the weighty questions that will return soon enough. The show of humor and
even joy in the face of death--both the impending fictional death of the *povre
Villon* and the actual confrontation with death witnessed earlier in the
poem--may either be taken as an act of self-deception (the illusory feeling of
well-being associated with drunkenness) or as a futile act of courage.

The City

The sites mentioned in the legacies, names which would be immediately
recognized by any of Villon's contemporaries, form a kind of itinerary
through mid-fifteenth-century Paris. Villon's route takes him through the
quarters of the city he knows best: the districts known for their taverns and
brothels, the Cemetery of the Innocents (where various illicit activities took
place), the Ile de la Cité, the neighborhood of the Sorbonne. The *Testament*
is very much a poem of the city, and Villon, like Baudelaire, finds a place in
his poetry for even the most sordid quarters of Paris.[5]

The urban setting of the *Testament* diverges from the traditional pastoralism typically associated with medieval French lyric poetry. Early lyric genres such as the *chanson d'amour* and the *pastourelle* are generally framed in rustic settings; nature continues to play an important role in the fifteenth century, in the poetry of Charles d'Orléans, for example. The poet's mood is often compared or contrasted with natural phenomena, the changing of the seasons, burgeoning plant life, the singing of birds. The *Testament*, on the other hand, is placed in a distinctively urban milieu where streets and shops replace fields and trees, and the noise of commerce replaces the song of birds.

One might explain the prominence of the city in the *Testament* by the fact that Villon belongs to a line of "bourgeois" poets such as Colin Muset, Rutebeuf, Eustache Deschamps, who seek inspiration elsewhere than in the beauty of the country. But the ties that link the *Testament* to the poetry of the *trouvères* are stronger than they may at first appear. Both share, for instance, an intensely lyrical quality, a profoundly introspective orientation. Both attempt in some respect to portray the dualistic character of human nature. Both devote a good deal of attention to suffering, with the *trouvères* emphasizing mental pain, while Villon more often focuses on physical hardship.

The presence of the city in the *Testament*, although it may well be connected with a certain poetic tradition, has a much more immediate explanation. Villon's poem represents, among other things, a journey into past, a past that is inextricably attached to the city of Paris. Because the journey takes place within the poet's mind, the appearance of occasional landmarks--a tavern sign, a church, a famous building--provides little guidance to the reader trying to chart his course. Villon is not really taking us through Paris, but rather through the labyrinth of his memory in which disconnected images of the city may be glimpsed.

The Reemergence of Death

One of the first bequests listed in the *Testament* is a rondeau given to Ythier Marchant, probably a friend from Villon's student days, in memory of Marchant's deceased mistress. The piece was later put to music by an anonymous fifteenth-century composer:

> Mort, j'appelle de ta rigueur,
> Qui m'as ma maistresse ravie,
> Et n'es pas encore assouvie
> Se tu ne me tiens en langeur. (978-981)

> (Death I appeal your harshness
> Having robbed me of my mistress
> You remain unsatisfied
> Waiting for me to languish too).

The rondeau, referring to the actual demise of a young woman with whom Villon was quite possibly personally acquainted, brings death a little closer to the poet, and serves as a somber reminder of the theme so prevalent earlier in the poem. Following this brief moment of solemnity, however, any serious consideration of death is suppressed for more than seven hundred verses. The legacy section, full of vitality and humor but also marked by anger and violence, constitutes an attempted escape from the overbearing issues that have been initially confronted, but not yet resolved. The legacies provide Villon with an excuse to indulge in a kind of verbal debauchery, an indecent excess, an adventure in materialism and sensuality. During this bewildering extravaganza, it is Villon, as we have seen, who takes and maintains control over his world. Death no longer looms menacingly over him--it is he who threatens others with death, handing out nooses and a lethal block of ice.

Eventually, however, the ploy begins to fail, and death reenters the poem. Warning his *compaigns de galle* ("comrades in revels") to attend to their spiritual health, Villon prophesies a bad end for those who do not heed his advice:

> Gardez vous tous de ce mau hasle
> Qui noircist les gens quant sont mors. (1722-1723)

> (Watch out all of you for that dry rot
> That turns men black when they're dead).

The word *hasle* actually signifies the light and heat of the sun. At one level Villon is evoking the sight of exposed, blackened corpses left hanging from the gallows (a medieval custom intended for public edification). But the image also implies an even graver consequence, for the *hasle* of which the poet warns his companions may also be taken as the infernal heat that awaits the unrepentant sinner. The world one enters through death, the world whose presence has already been suggested in "Ballade des dames du temps jadis" and graphically depicted in the "Ballade pour prier Nostre Dame" now returns to haunt the poem.

Shortly after this stern warning to the *compaigns de galle* and a subsequent commentary on the futility of pursuing worldly pleasure, the poet's attention drifts to the Cemetery of the Innocents where unearthed bones, disinterred while opening new graves, were a common sight in Villon's day:

> Quant je considere ces testes
> Entassees en ces charniers,
> Tous furent maistres des requestes,
> Au moins de la Chambre aux Deniers. (1744-1747)

> (When I consider these skulls
> Piled up in the boneyards
> Every one was Finance Minister
> At least of the Royal Treasury).

Early in the *Testament* Villon reflected on death as a painful physical experience waiting at the end of every life. Now, contemplating a pile of skulls, he resumes his mediation, focusing this time on the separation of body and spirit, and the continuation of spiritual existence after death:

> Or sont ilz mors, Dieu ait leurs ames!
> Quant est des corps, ilz sont pourris. (1760-1761)

> (They are dead God rest their souls[6]
> Their bodies have rotted away).

With the stark and sobering image of skulls lying on the cemetery ground fully exposed to view, the frenzied pace of the legacies is momentarily broken, and the carnival atmosphere quickly recedes as the poem undergoes a radical change of tone. The voice we hear now, suddenly devoid of flippancy and mirth, is preaching an eloquent sermon on the follies of worldly wealth and pleasure, and the illusory nature of non-spiritual values. (Villon has selected an appropriate site for his sermon. The Cemetery of the Innocents was frequently chosen by preachers as an ideal setting for their message.) The dramatic intrusion of death into the *Testament* and the

simultaneous shift of poetic register, sudden though they may appear, do not
come totally unannounced. Both in title and in theme Villon's poem is, after
all, a work that reserves an important place for death. Given the significance
of death in the first part of the *Testament* and the futility of its attempted
suppression in the legacy section, it is inevitable that the theme should
resurface before the end of the poem.

The series of bequests, however, has not yet ended. Civil judges
become the next victims of Villon's will as he condemns them through
extended antiphrasis. Exactly how the poem has passed from skulls to
judges we can only surmise. Perhaps the link occurs in the passage from
divine to human justice. At any rate, just as Villon appears to have
successfully eluded the question of death, and seems prepared to embark on
another digressionary excursion into his past, a familiar specter reemerges
in an unlikely place. Villon's gift to Jacquet Cardon, a wealthy cloth
merchant, is a *bergonnette* (a light song often recited by children) which, the
poet specifies, is to be sung to a popular tune of the day. The *bergonnette*
was supposedly written originally for a Marion de la Peautarde, about
whom we know nothing, but seems well suited to Villon himself. Instead of
the playful lyrics which one would expect to find in a song of this genre, we
encounter a somber recollection of imprisonment, a protest against
Fortune, and a prayer for the singer's soul containing a line from an
inscription on the wall of the Innocents:[7]

> Plaise a Dieu que l'ame ravie
> En soit lassus en sa maison. (1793-1794)

> (May it please God to gather
> My ravished soul into his house).

Even the song of children is haunted by thoughts of suffering and death. The
Testament will quickly resume its bantering tone, but now a tension clearly
exists between the frivolity of the mock will and the solemnity surrounding
the confrontation of death, a tension which will progressively intensify
throughout the remainder of the poem.

Soon after the *bergonnette*, Villon leaves a group of facetious gifts to
amans enfermés ("sick lovers") along with the stipulation that they recite a
prayer:

Pour l'ame du povre Villon (1811)

(For the soul of poor Villon).

From now on, Villon's encounter with death will become less abstract and more personal in nature. He is already beginning to envision his bodily absence and his spiritual continuation.

CHAPTER SEVEN: The Degeneration of Love
(Verses 1378-1405, 1473-1506, 1591-1627)

Among the ballads inserted into the legacy section of the *Testament* three pieces take up the theme of sexuality which is treated at length in the "Double Ballade." In this trilogy we witness a deterioration of love, or, to put it differently, the introduction of a foreign element into the *Testament*, and the gradual assimilation of this element into the poem through a process of metamorphosis.

The ballad left to Robert d'Estouteville, Provost of Paris, stands out from the *Testament* for a number of reasons. It is the only lyric insertion written completely in the courtly register of the traditional French love lyric, the *chanson d'amour*. The opening lines of the poem typify the emphasis on nature imagery which dominates the poem:

> Au poinct du jour, que l'esprevier s'esbat,
> Meu de plaisir et par noble coustume (1378-1379)

> (At daybreak when the sparrow hawk disports
> Made to soar by joy and noble custom).

The falcon in flight, symbolizing the lover's soaring spirit, calls to mind a similar image from a famous song by the twelfth-century troubadour, Bernart de Ventadorn:

> Can vei la aluzeta mover
> de joi sas alas contral rai

> (When I see the lark moving
> its wings in joy against the light).[1]

As the opening verses suggest, Villon's ballad is a brief ascent from the *Testament*, for both in style and theme the piece elevates itself from the rest of the poem, like the prayer written for the poet's mother. In the grand tradition of the troubadours and the *trouvères*, Villon celebrates the ideal of *fin'amors*, love in its most pure and noble form. But while *fin'amors* is normally associated with some obstacle such as the restrictions of marital fidelity, the sentiment celebrated in this poem is a conjugal love that knows no restraint.

With its lofty language and ideals, the "Ballade pour Robert d'Estouteville" contrasts sharply with its poetic matrix, the legacies, which in tone and content is anything but courtly, and at first the poem appears completely out of place in the *Testament*. One can partially explain this apparent incongruity by assuming that this piece is one of several lyric poems antedating the composition of the *Testament*. Still, it is difficult to justify the precise placement of the ballad, other than by pointing to the seemingly random distribution of Villon's eclectic collection of gifts. The placement of Robert's poem prior to the "Contreditz de Franc Gontier" and the "Ballade de la Grosse Margot," on the other hand, fits a pattern which will soon become apparent.

One striking feature of this ballad is that it contains in its opening verse the only image of daylight to be found in the whole of the *Testament*: "Au poinct du jour..." In this work of over two thousand verses with its extraordinary lexical range, the words for "sun," "light," "shine" are totally absent. Firelight, occasionally present, generally carries connotations of infernal punishment or bodily warmth. The *Testament* is literally a dark poem. This obscurity suits the dim streets of medieval Paris through which the poet's memory wanders, and also gives the poem a nocturnal quality. Since the *Testament* is an interior journey, one which takes the traveler closer to death, darkness provides a natural ambiance. However, at this point in the poem night is dispelled by a vibrant dawn associated with the flight of a bird, the mating song of another, the awakening of desire in the lover--all joyful signs of vitality.

The one appearance of light, the universal symbol of all that is good-- life, purity, health, happiness, spiritual joy and enlightenment—coincides with the single example of true love to be found in the *Testament*. Having reduced heterosexual love to simple lust, a dangerous appetite expressing itself in manipulation or deceit and capable of provoking extreme violence, Villon has seemingly banished love once and for all from his poem. Now, however, he allows it to re-enter in a new and purified form. Here is one answer to the problem of human solitude, a problem the *Testament* has already squarely and painfully confronted: not to violate nature and divine commandment, but to live in harmony with them, not to destroy but to create:

Si ne pers pas la graine que je sume
En vostre champ, quant le fruit me ressemble.
Dieu m'ordonne que le fouÿsse et fume. (1398-1400)

(The seed I sow is never lost
In your field for the fruit resembles me
God commands I till it and make it bear).

The sexual act, restored to its biological function, becomes a means of regeneration as well as the physical embodiment of the husband's love for his wife. Earlier in the ballad Robert envisions death as the limit of his love for Ambroise:

Dame serez de mon cuer sans debat
Entierement, jusques mort me consume. (1386-1387)

(Dominion you shall have over my heart
Entirely until death takes me).

Now we see the means by which a living sign of the love will survive the lover. Because the "sowing of the field" is ordained by God, the conception of the child, the union of man and woman required for this conception, and even the desire necessary to accomplish this union, all become part of a holy design. Villon has raised love from the depths of degradation to the highest level of aspiration. He has transformed the obscene into the sacred. Both the "Ballade pour prier Nostre Dame" and the "Ballade pour Robert d'Estouteville" form moments of spiritual elevation, one through prayer, the other through love. Both poems also afford Villon the rare opportunity to temporarily set aside his own preoccupations in order to imagine the world through the eyes of another. These ballads, therefore, mark a double transcendence, rising not only above the banality of daily existence, but also above the confines of the self.

Villon's sensitivity to the beauty and harmony of this perfect conjugal relationship only underscores his exclusion from the intimate scene he has just created. If Robert has been given an antidote to the sickness of solitude, the remedy will not work or is not available for Villon. Immediately after this brief lyric interlude, the will reverts to its familiar mocking tone. The praise of conjugal love is followed shortly by Villon's "recipe" for frying *langues envieuses* (1422-1456). A mere sixteen verses separate some of the loftiest and vilest language to be found in the *Testament*.

The "Contreditz de Franc Gontier"

The "Ballade pour Robert d'Estouteville" and the sexual jokes scattered throughout Villon's legacies illustrate the two poles of the medieval attitude toward sex. Writers tend either to lower physical desire to its crudest possible form, or elevate it to the level of an almost spiritual longing. In such fifteenth-century prose works as *Les quinze joyes de mariage* and *Les cent nouvelles nouvelles* (and earlier, in the *fabliaux*) sexual episodes furnish a wealth of material for coarse humor and didactic commentaries. Sex, as treated by the *esprit gaulois*, is little more than an off-color joke. Concurrent with this farcical approach exists a diametrically opposed view of human sexuality exalting the carnal experience as the highest expression of *fin'amors*. Neither the *gaulois* nor the *courtois* tradition produced much literature that could be accurately termed erotic. One presents sex with slapstick humor, while the other dwells more on the lover's state of mind than on the fulfillment of his desire.

Villon's treatment of human sexuality, closely allied with the *esprit gaulois*, remains rather heavy-handed, with the notable exception of the poem just examined. Between the two extremes of debasing desire and *fin'amors*, however, we are allowed to glimpse a sexual scene which, if not truly erotic by modern standards, at least can be described as highly sensual in nature. In the ballad commonly known as the "Contreditz de Franc Gontier" Villon ridicules the pastoral life praised in Philippe de Vitry's "Dit de Franc Gontier," a poem that enjoyed wide popularity in Villon's day. The *chanoine* of the first verse may refer to Philippe de Vitry, himself a canon; Sidoine is a character from a fifteenth-century work of fiction:

> Sur mol duvet assis, ung gras chanoine,
> Lez ung brasier, en chambre bien natee,
> A son costé gisant dame Sidoine,
> Blanche, tendre, polie et attintee,
> Boire ypocras, a jour et a nuytee. (1473-1477)

> (A plump canon lounging on an eiderdown
> Near the fire in a thickly carpeted room
> Lady Sidonia stretching out beside him
> White, delectable, glistening, primped
> sipping mulled wine by day and by night).

Si j'ayme et sers la belle de bon hait,
M'en devez vous tenir ne vil ne sot?
Elle a en soy des biens a fin souhait.
Pour son amour sains bouclier et passot. (1591-1594)

(Because I love and gladly serve this woman
Must you call me degenerate and a fool?
She has something for the nicest taste
For her love I strap on shield and dagger).

We quickly learn that the knight is a pimp, the lady is a whore, and their court is actually a brothel. Love again is humbled, as Villon assimilates it into the world of the *Testament*. To some, Villon's farcical version of courtly love may appear deeply cynical. It would be unfair, however, to assume that the "Ballade de la Grosse Margot" refutes the possibility of true love. Instead, the poem should be read as a sequel to the "Ballade pour Robert d'Estouteville" and the "Contreditz de Franc Gontier." Each of these three poems depicts one level of heterosexual relations. Villon's appearance in the last poem simply indicates the level with which he chooses to associate himself. For all its coarseness, obscenity, and violence, the last poem of the series is the one which portrays the most human relationship. Robert communicates his love for Ambroise in abstract or metaphorical language, and we never actually see her responding to his love. The canon and Sidoine, while going through the motions of physical love, merely serve to exemplify the purely sensual aspect of sexuality, never emerging as distinct personalities. In the case of Villon and Margot, however, we see two people reacting to each other in a dynamic and spontaneous manner.[3] The result is a comical and fully credible scene.

In the "Ballade pour Robert d'Estouteville" we are made to feel the lover's longing for union, but this yearning is identified with mating birds and fallow fields. In the "Contraditz" we see desire take the form of human bodies, but these bodies, being in a sense hypothetical, never acquire any individual identity. It is not until the "Ballade de la Grosse Margot" that we see two actual human beings emotionally relating to each other, showing anger, hatred, mistrust, weakness, playfulness, lust. The evolution of the sexual theme through these poems may be described not only as a brutalization of *fin'amors*, but also a humanization of this idealized and etherealized vision of male-female relations.

The "Ballade de la Grosse Margot" deserves attention for another reason. What are we to make of the fact that in the only scene of the *Testament* in which Villon presents an extended dramatization of his relationship with another person, that person turns out to be a prostitute? In one sense Villon's "lady" ideally complements her prince, both having been relegated to the margin of society. The scene also offers a graphic and humorous depiction of Villon's victimization, a constant theme of his poem:

> Et, au resveil, quant le ventre luy bruit,
> Monte sur moy, que ne gaste son fruit.
> Soubz elle geins, plus qu'un aiz me fait plat. (1616-1618)

> (And when we wake and her belly calls
> She gets on top so not to spoil her fruit
> I groan underneath pressed flatter than a plank).

After this farcical bedroom scene Villon closes the poem with a revealing comment on his relationship with Margot:

> L'ung vault l'autre; c'est a mau rat mau chat. (1624)

> (Like unto like, bad rat bad cat).

The verb *vault* may be translated as "equals"; Villon is establishing not a comparison but an equivalence: Margot=Villon. By equating himself with his female counterpart, Villon in effect becomes a kind of prostitute. This does not mean that he literally sells his body, but rather that he, like Margot, is personally acquainted with the depths of degradation to which human nature is capable of sinking. He describes himself in the conclusion of the poem as *paillart* (1622), a word that signifies either "dirty" or "despicable," a strongly derogatory term in either case.

Like the "Ballade pour prier Nostre Dame," this ballad also bears in its *envoi* the poet's acrostic signature. It is no accident that Villon leaves his name precisely in the places that might well be considered the highest point of the *Testament*, a beautiful and moving prayer for intercession, and the lowest point, a scene of debauchery and personal debasement. Nor is it an accident that in Villon's first acrostic signature several sacred names appear, while in the second we find the word *ordure*, "filth." Confronted with the dramatic contrast presented by these two poems, one may point to the paradoxical nature of the *Testament* and to the inconsistencies of its author. But the implications of this contrast extend far beyond the boundaries of the *Testament*, embracing the struggle of the spirit and the flesh with which the medieval mind was so preoccupied. The *Testament*, like the humanity it mirrors, contains elements of sublime spirituality as well as stubborn materialism. The poem to this point has continually oscillated between the two extremes. Now, however, these conflicting perspectives will gradually merge as the end of the poem and the end of the dying testator begin to draw near.

CHAPTER EIGHT: Final Preparations (Verses 1844-1995)

Now that all the bequests have been made, Villon turns his attention to the last few remaining formalities: provisions for the execution of the will, the choice of a burial site, the composition of an epitaph, the appointment of pallbearers, and other necessary details. Jehan Calais, a notary of the Châtelet charged with verifying wills and a man whom Villon admits he has never met, is named to interpret the will and adjudicate any disputes that may arise. Villon gives the notary practically unlimited power to construe and even modify the document:

> De le gloser et commenter,
> De le diffinir et descripre,
> Diminuer ou augmenter,
> De le canceller et prescripre. (1852-1855)

> (To gloss and annotate it
> To define and clarify it
> To shorten and lengthen it
> To void it and scratch it out).

Playfully handling terms borrowed from the semantic fields of scholastic and legal terminology, Villon loosens and reinvigorates a normally rigid and lifeless form of language. At the same time he makes us aware of the vulnerability of the written word. Just as the will must be interpreted after the testator's death in order to be properly carried out, the literary text must be continually interpreted and reinterpreted in order to remain valid. We should take Villon's instructions to his notary as a warning, for it is we who have now become the real executors of Villon's will, glossing, annotating, and defining his text. Although this act of interpretation is incumbent upon each new generation of "executors," we must remember, as Villon subtly reminds us, that this process entails a risk of distortion or even misrepresentation.

Parodying a common testamentary provision concerning the disposition of a bequest in the event of an heir's death, Villon envisions a different eventuality:

Et s'aucun, dont n'ay congnoissance,
Estoit allé de mort a vie (1860-1861)

(And if unknown to me an heir
Has passed from death into life).

The words "de mort a vie" appear in medieval French literature as a verbal formula traditionally applied to Christ.[1] This religiously weighted phrase announces a series of Christ images that occur, concealed by comic effects, in the concluding ballad of the *Testament*. In broadest terms, the movement of Villon's poem has been one of life toward death. Now the phrase "de mort a vie" suggests an extension of the same movement beyond death to an enduring life.

To the stipulation that his sepulchre be located in the convent of Saint Avoye (patron saint of the *dévoyés*, the black sheep, whom she was believed capable of leading back to a righteous life), he adds a further request:

Et, affin que chascun me voie,
Non pas en char, mais en painture,
Que l'on tire mon estature
D'ancre, s'il ne coustait trop chier. (1870-1873)

(And so everyone may see me
Not in the flesh but in painting
Have my full-length portrait done
In ink if there's money for that).

If we take the *estature d'ancre* to be the verbal self-portrait contained in the *Testament*, then it becomes clear that Villon has already fulfilled his own request. This reading is reinforced by the fact that in the other two occurrences of *ancre* to be found in Villon's poetry the word is specifically connected to the act of writing a will.[2] Since we cannot see him *en char*, we can only see a picture of him *en painture*. To rearrange the famous phrase from the Gospel of John, the flesh becomes word.

Having named his resting place, Villon now proceeds to specify the details of his epitaph:

Soit escript en lettre assez grosse,
Et qui n'auroit point d'escriptoire,
De charbon ou de pierre noire. (1878-1880)

(Inscribed in rather large letters
Lacking something to write with
Use charcoal or a lump of coal).

Although the primary meaning of *grosse* in this context is apparently "large," the word can also signify "common" or "vulgar."[3] The inscription that Villon envisions scribbled in charcoal over his grave take the form of a kind of graffiti, and the epitaph does in fact contain the kind of obscene term (*cul*) that one would expect to find in such a crude inscription. Again we see an act of debasement, this time self-imposed. Making a mockery of his epitaph, Villon is faithfully following his practice of desecrating that which his society regards with reverence. But the graffiti on the grave may also represent a deeper revolt. If the tomb symbolizes death, the epitaph symbolizes man's submission to death, his acceptance of the inevitable. Villon's inscription, scrawled in large black letters, insults the sanctity of the grave, and evokes laughter in the face of death. As with the final gulp of wine at the end of the poem, it may be taken as a gesture of defiance.

In the epitaph Villon cites his full name for the first and only time in the *Testament*. Death has reduced the omnipotent benefactor of the legacy section to a humble cleric by the name of François Villon:

Ung povre petit escollier,
Qui fut nommé Françoys Villon. (1886-1887)

(A poor obscure scholar
Who was known as François Villon).

Referring to himself in the third person, and looking momentarily beyond his death, Villon begins to prepare his departure, and announces the eulogy to be delivered by an anonymous voice at the end of the poem. The words *petit escollier*, translated above as "obscure scholar," literally mean a "small schoolboy." The *Testament* moves simultaneously in a forward direction toward the poet's death, and backward through his past, the future and past merging in the epitaph that looks backward and forward at once.

The image painted by the epitaph, the inscription that will supposedly fix his memory for all posterity, is that of a man completely stripped-- stripped of love, possessions (all of which he claims to have given away), stripped even of the hair on his face and head. But the pathos of the image is undercut by an ironic bit of courtly language:

Qu'amours occist de son raillon (1885)

(One love's arrow struck down),

and a reminder that the poet's tomb is to be housed in the *sollier* (1884), "upper room," of a convent. Villon clearly intends to leave a mock epitaph on a mock tomb. The prayer quoted in the inscription, containing the word *cul* as well as a traditional liturgical phrase, is also a mockery. At another level, however, Villon is conceiving his death, his grave, the memory he will leave behind, is requesting that a requiem prayer be recited for his soul, is confronting the most difficult and anxiety-filled questions facing every intelligent human being, all beneath the mask of humor. The association of death and humor, moreover, is completely normal. Jokes about death are as old as jokes about sex, and both, as it is well known, betray an understandable uneasiness and insecurity. If Villon is to introduce his own encounter with death into the *Testament*, and still keep the distance he has attempted to maintain between the poem and the personal experience it reflects, then he has no choice but to approach the subject through the means of humor, even to the extent of self-deprecation.

The final preparations for death fail to depress the resilient spirit of the dying testator. Instead they provide him with a last opportunity for a little satirical sport as he appoints the bell ringers and his executors. An obscene pun is tossed at a former schoolmate, Thomas Tricot, now a priest. Just as the flippant tone of the legacy section seems about to reassert itself, Villon cuts short the string of jokes with a reference to physical suffering:

Trop plus mal me font qu'onques mais
Barbe, cheveulx, penil, sourcis.
Mal me presse, temps desormais
Que crie a toutes gens mercis. (1964-1967)

(Worse than ever they're killing me
My beard, hair, crotch, and eyebrows
Pain closes in, it's high time now
To cry everyone's pardon).

With this reminder of the agony of dying, the poem revolves back to the grim reality confronted in Villon's painfully graphic description of the *agonisant* (313-328). The attempt to elude the ultimate threat of death has failed, and the vague awareness of mortality perceptible in the opening verse of the *Testament* returns with greater definition and intensity as the final moments of the poem and of the dying protagonist coincide.

In an act of confession the writer of the will, pressed by death and with little time remaining, focuses his last thoughts on those he has wronged, enumerating various groups of people in the ballad with the refrain, "Je crye a toutes gens mercis" (1968-1995). Yet when we observe the procession to whom Villon's plea is addressed, we find very few of those he has maligned in the poem. Members of several religious orders are included, but nowhere does Villon refer to the magistrates, the municipal officials, the wealthy bourgeois, and the others who have borne the brunt of his abuse. Instead we see mainly people of the street, especially those who occupy a marginal social position: prostitutes, thieves, brawlers, itinerant entertainers, jesters, actors. These are the people Villon knows best, the ones who form his true social milieu, and it is to them that he now turns before departing. The poem which began in the privacy of personal memories, and which has retained a highly introspective orientation now moves into the street to embrace a colorful array of human figures, practically all of whom are, like Villon, alienated to some degree from their society. The sense of intense isolation evident throughout the *Testament* briefly yields to a sense of communion and solidarity. At the same time, the introspective nature of the poem does not totally disappear. In reaching out to the monk, the thief, the jester, the actor, the rejected lover, Villon is also reaching out to and gathering together the various constituent elements of his total personality.

The apparent humility and good will of Villon's "confession" is undermined by the ballad's ending in which the poet curses those who kept him jailed in the prison at Meung-sur-Loire. Villon cannot ask forgiveness for his harsh verbal treatment of his jailers. On the contrary, he assails them with some of the most vehement language of the *Testament*:

> Qu'on leur froisse les quinze costes
> De gros mailletz, fors et massis,
> De plombees et telz pelotes. (1992-1994)

> (Let their fifteen ribs be mauled
> With big hammers heavy and strong
> And lead weights and that kind of balls).

The memory of his recent experience in prison which opened the poem is obviously still quite fresh in Villon's mind. While previous allusions to Thibault d'Aussigny and Meung-sur-Loire remain couched in sarcastic terms, Villon makes his final assault in uncharacteristically blunt, unequivocally violent language. Having fully vented his anger and purged himself of resentment, he returns to his plea for pardon. The cursing of the jailers, coming at the end of a petition for forgiveness, underscores the fallibility of the petitioner. In the awesome moment at which he should be making peace with the world before departing, he cannot find within his heart the will to forgive his enemies. Still, the final verse of the ballad, and of the will proper, suggests an attitude of reconciliation, humility, and penance.

Taken literally and within the context of the whole poem, the phrase "Je crye a toutes gens mercis" incorporates a larger meaning. "Je crye" represents the entire verbal act of the *Testament*, the crying out, the urgent demand for attention. Those to whom Villon cries out, "toutes gens," are not only those he knows personally, but all those who read his poem, all those who hear his cry. And the plea he makes to us is that we, his readers, grant him "mercis," compassion and understanding, *miséricorde*. Read in this manner, the refrain restates a verse of Villon's famous "Ballade des pendus:"

N'ayez les cuers contre nous endurcis (2)

(Don't let your hearts harden against us).

It is significant that the last utterance of the dying voice dictating the will is a word charged with religious implications, and whose meanings touch the very core of Christianity. As "mercy," "pity," or "compassion" *mercis* encompasses the essential qualities characterizing Christian behavior. As "forgiveness" or "grace" it embodies the hope for salvation. The man who has given so much of himself--his poetry, his emotion, his intellect--who, according to his epitaph, has given all he has, ends his testament in a gesture of supplication, finally asking, even pleading, to receive.

**CHAPTER NINE: Three Readings of the Final Ballad
(Verses 1996-2023)**

The *Testament* closes with an epilogue in the form of a eulogy delivered by a disembodied voice. Like the epitaph of which it is an extension, the final ballad succinctly summarizes the life of the deceased, stressing the hardships and humiliations he was forced to endure. Because of its function as a conclusion to the *Testament*, and the privileged status it acquires by affording Villon an ultimate opportunity to comment on the preceding text, the closing ballad merits scrupulous attention. The epilogue offers us, in fact, a number of clues to help decipher the meaning of this mysterious work. According to which clues we collect, we may read the ballad and the long poem it concludes in at least three different ways. Moreover, these readings are not mutually exclusive, but rather superimposed, each interpreting the poem at a different level.

The Victim

Adding an obscene twist to a stock rhetorical device lifted from courtly tradition, the speaker of the eulogy describes Villon's death as an act of martyrdom:

> Car en amours mourut martir
> Ce jura il sur son couillon. (2001-2002)
>
> (For he died a martyr to love
> This he swore on his testicle).

The physical loss implied by the singular, *son couillon*, reinforces and concretizes the victimization which the preceding verse renders in more abstract imagery. Villon, who has worn so many masks throughout his poem, has chosen for his exit the mask of the martyred lover that he first tried on five years earlier in the *Lais*.[1] The final ballad culminates a series of images portraying the *povre Villon* as a pathetic victim. The martyr, as we learn, lived in a state of perpetual exile, leaving pitiful traces of his presence wherever he went:

> Tant que, d'icy a Roussillon,
> Brosse n'y a ne brossillon
> Qui n'eust, ce dit il sans mentir,
> Ung lambeau de son cotillon. (2007-2010)

> From here to Roussillon
> There isn't a shrub or a bush
> That didn't get, he truly speaks,
> A shred from his back).

Not only has the *povre Villon* parted with all his possessions, but he has even left behind his *cotillon*, the tunic worn as an undergarment, parcelled out in shreds and leaving its owner in a virtual state of nakedness. Now the anonymous voice describes the martyr's end, depicting in vivid terms the moment of his death:

> Qui plus, en mourant, mallement
> L'espoignoit d'Amours l'esguillon;
> Plus agu que le ranguillon
> D'ung baudrier luy faisoit sentir. (2014-2017)

> (What's worse, as he died, sorely
> The spur of love pricked into him
> Sharper than the buckle-tongue
> Of a baldric he could feel it).

Again the abstract is conceptualized in graphic terms. The adverb *mallement* can also be read as *mâle-ment*, "in male fashion."[2] The epitaph states that the poet was killed by a *raillon*, a word sometimes loosely translated as "arrow," but actually designating the bolt of a crossbow, a short, square-headed missile. The image of a buckle-tongue strongly connotes phallic penetration (as Kinnell's felicitous translation of verse 2015 implies), and combined with the phallic nature of the *raillon* and the reading of *mâle-ment* suggests a novel form of martyrdom which elicits our astonishment:

> C'est de quoy nous esmerveillon (2018)

> (And that is what we marvel at).

The theme of victimization culminates in a brutal sexual assault.[3]

For Villon to take his proper place among the other martyrs of love, he must first die a martyr's death. But what are we to make out of this final mockery? Summoned by the bells, we have dutifully arrived at the poet's funeral dressed in the appropriate garb for commemorating a martyr's death (1998-2000). As we listen to the eulogy, we reverently await the re-enactment of the "martyr's" final moments. And now, as the anticipated moment arrives, we suddenly realize that we are watching a farce. It is not only the hapless hero of the poem who is being mocked, but we ourselves, as we stand solemnly and properly in our vermilion, watching this unexpected and totally undignified scene.

The last gesture of the moribund martyr is one of despair:

Sachiez qu'il fist au departir:
Ung traict but de vin morillon. (2021-2022)

(Hear what he did as he left
He took a long swig of dead-black wine).

In the face of a long series of personal misfortunes, the drinking of the wine represents an act of desperation, an attempt to escape the pain and shame which have just been inflicted. It is the exaggerated gesture of a puppet manipulated into grotesque positions by the smiling puppeteer. The note of tragedy, for which we have been so carefully prepared, never rings. Instead, the last sound echoing from the world of the *Testament*, after all the raucous noises have subsided, is one of haunting laughter.

The Victor

If the final ballad may be read as a fitting slapstick finale to a long tragicomic farce, it may be taken with equal validity as the heroic conclusion to a tensely dramatic struggle. Throughout the *Testament* we have followed the conflict between the two primal forces of life and death. At one extreme the poem moves through the painful motions of the *danse macabre*, lamenting the brevity and fragility of human existence, evoking scenes of cemeteries, boneyards, tombs, deathbeds. At the other extreme, the poem moves to the rhythm of life, brimming with humor, gaiety, and vitality. Fluctuating constantly between the force of life and the force of death, the *Testament* finally succeeds in fusing the two. For although the closing ballad depicts a scene of death and invokes the dead, it also exudes laughter and life.

The epilogue of the *Testament* can hardly be said to bear no relation whatsoever to Villon's life as we know it. The references to destitution, banishment, and physical abuse all correspond in some degree to biographical fact. Beneath the obvious travesty of the final ballad lies a core of truth without which the poem would drift meaninglessly detached from the rest of the work. The heroism of the closing moments of the *Testament* consists in the poet's will to rise above his suffering through an act of self-mockery. Death will break Villon just as we have seen it break his effigy, but the *esprit* of the poem, reflecting the spirit of the man, will not be destroyed.

In speaking of himself in the third person, Villon separates himself into the observer and the observed, the *je* and the *il*, one deceased and one who continues to live. In so doing, he has in a sense managed to outlive himself, conquering death. At the same time, the voice of the eulogy, speaking for the now voiceless martyr, comes to us in effect from the other side of the grave. Even before he has died, Villon is already addressing us from the realm of the dead.

The Other Victim

Still another reading of the ballad points to a different hero, and consequently a different ending. Whether a mask deliberately assumed by the poet, or a figure unconsciously summoned, an image of the crucified Christ may be seen, without unduly straining the imagination, in the final verses of the *Testament*.[4] Moreover, the connection between the poet and Christ is one for which the reader of the poem should not be totally unprepared. First, there is the matter of Villon's age--thirty years at the writing of the *Testament*. More important is Villon's relationship with Society. Constantly coming into conflict with civil and ecclesiastical authority, he too was something of an outcast, moving in a milieu considered dangerous by the social establishment. Also, Villon's self-portrayal is that of a sacrificial victim, a martyr, a man who has received far harsher treatment than he deserves, yet who claims he is prepared to give up his life if his death would benefit the *bien publicque*, the "common good" (121). Finally, the phrase, "Car en amours mourut martir" (2001) applies equally well to both martyrs, one of whom died for a higher form of love than did the other.

To see in athe shredding of the martyr's tunic, left behind on every bush "d'icy a Roussillon" (2007), a parallel to the division of Christ's clothing among the Roman soldiers hardly requires an extraordinary leap of imagination. Whether carried out by human or natural agents, the distribution of clothing is accomplished in an equally random manner, leaving the victim to face his death in a state of virtual nakedness. But not completely naked:

> Il est ainsi et tellement,
> Quant mourut n'avoit qu'ung haillon. (2012-2013)

> (It was like this, so that
> By the time he died he had only a rag).

This poor excuse for a garment, according to popular belief and almost every late medieval painting of the scene, was Christ's only clothing on the cross.

One martyr is wounded by an arrow immediately prior to his death; the other is pierced by a lance immediately after his death. The last recorded act of the *povre Villon* and the last recorded act of Christ (according to the Gospel of John) are identical: the drinking of wine. The wine offered to the victims of crucifixion was a cheap soldier's drink; Villon, wishing to make his exit with a little class, treats himself to a *vin supérieur*. It is the act, however, and not the quality of the wine that should claim our attention. While the stripping of the garments, the *haillon*, the arrow wound may be individually construed as vague or fortuitous parallels to the Crucifixion, the consumption of wine as the final act preceding death cannot be so easily discounted, especially when taken in conjunction with the other evidence.

Clearly the type of wine, *morillon*, is not a random selection. First, appearing in the penultimate verse of the *Testament*, the word allows Villon to partially sign his work (*illon*). The word may also be taken, given the poet's frequent use of ellipsis, as a slight abbreviation of *mort Villon*. It is in usage as well as in name a sort of "death wine," a wine to be consumed at the moment of death. But also, perhaps, a wine to be consumed in memory of a death. The drinking of the wine, therefore, along with its other connotations, takes on a eucharistic function.

The word *morillon* in Villon's time was commonly associated with the color black, being used to designate either a black grape, a black duck, or a cloth of the same color.[5] The last color image of the *Testament* is one which is rich in symbolic significance and fittingly emblematic of the poem's duality. On one hand, black connotes despair, melancholy, death, and is, of course, the color of mourning. On the other hand, it symbolizes sleep, eternity, the womb, and also the fertility of the earth.[6] In the context of the *Testament* the image of blackness marks both an ending and a beginning.

The figure of Christ that emerges in the final ballad of Villon's poem suggests one answer, and perhaps, in the context of medieval thought, the only valid answer to the quest whose progress may be traced through the *Testament*. In the course of his will, Villon has methodically devalued various ideals to which men dedicate their lives. Material security and the acquisition of financial wealth (Jacques Cuer in his *riche tumbeau*) lose all meaning inside the darkness of the tomb. The *Belle Heaulmière*'s epicurean attitude toward life can hardly provide more than temporary relief from the crushing burden of mortality. Love, while it may work for Robert and Ambroise, causes more pain than happiness in the eyes of Villon. Human justice is a sham. Kindness and goodness are no match for cruelty and malice. Having revealed the fallibility and illusory nature of all these values, Villon is left with the only value that has resisted the derisive force of his poem. For all his anger, bitterness, and apparent scorn of social respectability, Villon never comes close to profaning the truly sacred. And it is only the truly sacred, in the end, which survives. The evocation of the Crucifixion may indicate, or at least suggest, that the persona of the *Testament* is moving toward a state of grace. By identifying the martyr of his poem with Christ on the cross, Villon elevates the suffering of the former, endowing it with new meaning.

The journey through the private space of the *Testament* ends then with a scene that one level represses past pain, injustice, and anguish by means of a comic device, while at another level redeeming these memories by placing them within a Christian context. The closing ballad which may appear at first reading to represent the nonsensical climax of a nightmarish passage through the darkest recesses of the human spirit, also contains a promise of restored meaning, a faint resurgence of hope, a tentative illumination, the prelude to another stage of the journey.

CONCLUSION

Why did Villon choose the form of a will for his most ambitious and important poetic effort? Having already experimented with the form five years earlier when he wrote the *Lais,* he was obviously well acquainted with its potential as a vehicle for irony and humor. The satirical testament, of course, was not invented by Villon who was only one of a long line of writers to try his hand at this literary convention.[1] His *Testament,* however, extends far beyond the traditional confines of the genre. To grasp the essence of Villon's poem, one must turn not to the literary tradition from which it evolved, but to the nature of fifteenth-century wills.

We tend today to think of a legal will as a rather dry document filled with legalistic language and technical detail. The medieval will, by contrast, had a much broader function, ordering the testator's spiritual as well as his material affairs, specifying the place of burial, requesting requiem masses, and containing a variety of religious formulas acknowledging the mortal limits of humanity, the necessity of penance, and summarizing the Christian creed. As Jean Englemann points out in his study of fifteenth-century French wills, these texts represent more than mere secular concerns:

> Les invocations pieuses si universelles et
> si développées qu'ils contiennent nour permettent
> de conclure, sans pouvoir être taxé d'exagération,
> qu'au point de vue purement formaliste, le testament
> du xve siècle est un acte riligieux.[2]

The fifteenth-century will, addressing all important aspects of a man's life, embracing both spiritual and worldly concerns, amounts to a kind of self-definition in the face of death. Approaching his certain end, the testator deliberately and coherently identifies that which he cherishes most in his life. In this sense the will represents a statement of values. This clarification of priorities inevitably results in a sharp distinction between spiritual life and secular life. The fifteenth-century will typically treats the religious matters at the outset before proceeding to mundane concerns, leaving no doubt as to where the priorities lie.

The *Testament*, in spite of its many digressions, is loosely framed within the form of a will, and in spite of its obvious burlesque elements, possesses, as this study has attempted to demonstrate, a definite religious aspect in its multi-faceted character. Like other great products of the late medieval period, *The Canterbury Tales, The Decameron, The Celestina,* for example, the *Testament* shows evidence of a didactic intention. By undercutting all temporal values in an act of wholesale destruction, the poem leaves only the spiritual values standing intact. Now that its creator is actually dead, the *Testament* acquires validity as a real will, and we may truthfully count ourselves among the heirs. Villon has left us not only his poetry and wit, but also his own understanding, at once deeply personal and deeply medieval, of the meaning of human existence.

A will looks simultaneously to the past and to the future, as does the *Testament*. From the opening verse of the work, the theme of time asserts its importance. In the course of the *Testament* Villon repeatedly attempts to situate his poem in time, working with two broad frames of reference. First, he locates the poem within what might be termed "personal time," setting it against an autobiographical background: his age, the recent experience of imprisonment, the distance that separates the present moment from his early youth. The second frame might be labeled "historical time": the year 1461, references to well-known people and events, past and present, that place the poem in a more objective temporal perspective. While the early section of the *Testament* looks primarily toward the past, the poem's conclusion, especially in the epitaph and eulogy, is oriented more toward the future. There are also moments in the poem that altogether transcend the concept of time. The "Ballade des dames du temps jadis," the "Ballade pour prier Nostre Dame," and the "Ballade pour Robert d'Estouteville" all lift themselves above the destructive flow of time, pointing to the eternal.

A last will and testament can hardly be described as an inherently humorous document. Yet Villon's poem cannot adequately be described without reference to its humor. Mockery becomes a potent weapon when wielded by Villon, and he uses it expertly and pitilessly against those he despises. More important, he knows how to mock himself, his poverty, his humiliations, his suffering. If the writing of the will with all that this act implies--the survey of a life, the meditation on death, and the anticipation of that which lies beyond death--if all this is no more than a sham in Villon's poem, then the *Testament*'s humor is shallow and facile. If, however, the will and all the difficult issues it raises can be taken seriously at some level, then Villon's humor acquires a different meaning. Faced with the inevitable certainty of his mortality, the poet laughs at the illusory nature of temporal existence. Like almost every other aspect of the *Testament*, this laugh is deeply equivocal. It is the cynical cackle of a dying old man, and the unrestrained mirth of a child radiating life. It both ridicules us and encourages us, derides our weaknesses while offering us a source of strength. Villon is both laughing at us and with us.

NOTES

Chapter One

[1] Villon was liberated from Thibaut's prison in October of 1461; he wrote the *Testament* in the winter of 1461-1462.

[2] August Longnon, ed. *Oeuvres de François Villon. Quatrième edition revue par Lucien Foulet* (Paris: Champion, 1932), verses 1-6. All subsequent citations from Villon's poetry are taken from this edition. All English translations are from *The Poems of François Villon* translated by Galway Kinnell. Copyright © 1965, 1977 by Galway Kinnell. Reprinted by permission of Houghton Mifflin Company.

[3] Returning to Paris after his release from Thibaut's prison, Villon was forced to go into hiding to avoid inquiries concerning his role in the robbery of the College of Navarre five years earlier.

[4] On October 2, 1461, Louis XI, the new king of France, passed through Meung, and since it was the custom to free all prisoners to commemorate a new king's first entry into a city, Villon was released at this time.

[5] The question of sincerity in the *Testament* has aroused considerable controversy. For further reading on the topic, see: Norris Lacy, "Villon in his Work: the *Testament* and the Problem of Personal Poetry," (in *L'Esprit Createur*, 17, 60-69) and William Calin, "Observations on Point of View and the Poet's Voice" (in *L'Esprit Createur*, 7, 180-187).

[6] Grace Frank dismisses Villon's declarations of penitence ("The Impenitence of François Villon," in *Romanic Review*, 37, 225-236). Janis Pallister, on the other hand, takes Villon's confessions more seriously ("Attrition and Contrition in the Poetry of François Villon," in *Romance Notes*, 11, 392-398).

[7] Job, 7, 6.

Chapter Two

[1] Pilate's words: John 19, 22.

[2] The *bourreletz* were fashionable headdresses worn by bourgeois women in the fifteenth century.

[3] The frontispiece of this book (described in the preface) presents one illustration of the *danse macabre*. For further information on the subject, see: Edelgard DuBruck, *The Theme of Death in French Poetry* (The Hague: Mouton, 1964), especially chapters 1-3.

[4]Spitzer judges the ballad following the "Ballade des dames du temps jadis," to be inferior, and suggests it may even have been written as a parody of the first ballad ("Etude ahistorique d'un texte: Ballade des dames du temps jadis" in in *Modern Language Quarterly*, 1, 7-22). However, Norris Lacy ("The Flight of Time: Villon's Trilogy of Ballades," in *Romance Notes*, 22, 353-358) and Paul Lonigan ("Villon's Triptych," in *Neuphilologische Mitteilungen*, 70, 611-623) both underscore the thematic unity of the trilogy.

[5]See David Kuhn's commentary of the poem in *La Poétique de François Villon* (Paris, 1967), pp. 77-97, for a fascinating discussion of the theme of fertility.

Chapter Three

[1]*Cotillon* - a tunic worn as an undergarment.

[2]The first stanza of "Les Contreditz de Franc Gontier," (1473-1482).

[3]For example, verses 273, 657, 1886, 1997.

[4]Genesis 3, 10.

[5]For a striking example of this artistic motif, see Marcel Thomas, *The Golden Age: Manuscript Painting at the Time of Jean, Duke of Berry* (New York: Braziller, 1979), p. 54.

Chapter Four

[1]The single exception is the "Ballade pour Robert d'Estouteville" (1378-1405) discussed in Chapter Seven.

[2]The explication of the "Double Ballade" is based on my article, "The Povre Villon and Other Martyred Lovers of the *Testament*," in *Neophilologus*, 64, 347-357.

Chapter Five

[1]To appreciate the extent to which Villon draws on the legal and religious language employed in actual fifteenth-century wills, one only has to compare his poem to a few of the documents contained in Alexandre Tuetey's *Testaments enregistrés au Parlement de Paris sous le règne de Charles VI* (Paris: Imprimerie Nationale, 1880).

[2]This chapter is largely based on my article, "An unexplored Acrostic in Villon's *Testament*," in Fifteenth-Century Studies, 6, 115-119. For additional commentaries on the "Ballade pour prier Nostre Dame," see Edelgard DuBruck's "Villon's Two Pleas for Absolution" (in *L'Esprit Createur*, 7, 188-196), and Karl Uitti's "A Note on Villon's Poetics" (in *Romance Philology*, 30, 187-192).

[3]For some reason, this acrostic signature has attracted relatively little critical attention. Uitti, in his excellent commentary of the ballad, includes the final verse of the *envoi* in the acrostic, reading VILLONE. He perceptively interprets the feminine form of Villon's name as an indication of union between mother and son, but says little more about the acrostic. Kuhn touches on the acrostic (pp. 59-60), and recognizes the pattern of "noms divins" on which it is based, but he mentions the pattern almost as a matter of incidental interest, and devotes little attention to its possible meanings.

[4]Verses 105, 178, 273-274, 417.

[5]For a detailed analysis of this stanza, see Rupert Pickens' "The Concept of the Feminine Ideal in Villon's *Testament*: Huitain 89," in *Studies in Philology*, 70, 42-50.

[6]943-949 and 1621-1626.

Chapter Six

[1]For a thorough, concise, and balanced commentary, I strongly recommend the edition of Jean Rychner and Albert Henry (see bibliography).

[2]Rychner and Henry consider the Longnon-Foulet transcription of verse 1024 to be defective, and give: "Quoy? que Marchant ot pour estat," a reading Kinnell has followed in his translation.

[3]The word *cornete* actually refers to an ornamental band of cloth attached to a hat.

[4]"A play on the verses from a hymn to the Virgin:
        Ave, decus virginum,
        Ave, salus hominum." (Kinnell, p. 236)

[5]For a discussion of the role of the city in Villon's poetry, see: Joseph Hayes, "Gothic Love and Death: François Villon and the City of Paris" (in *Journal of Popular Culture*, 11, 719-729).

[6] I prefer a more literal translation of "Dieu ait leurs ames": "May God preserve their souls," or literally, "May God have their souls."

[7] Thuasne III, 501.

Chapter Seven

[1] Frederick Goldin, *Lyrics of the Troubadours and Trouvères* (New York, 1973), p. 145.

[2] Philippe de Vitry's poem opens:

> Soubz feuille vert, sur herbe delictable,
> Sur ruy bruyant et sur clere fontaine,
> Trouvay fichee une borde portable.
> Ilec mengoit Gontier et dame Helaine. (Thuasne III, 396)

[3] Margot is one of the characters of the *Testament* whose identity remains a mystery. She was possibly the madam of a house of prostitution near the cloister of Notre Dame. In any case, it appears very likely that she, like the two prostitutes named immediately after the ballad, Marion and Jehanne, did actually exist. The veracity of the incident related in the poem, of course, is open to speculation.

Chapter Eight

[1] Thuasne III, 518.

[2] Prens ancre tost, plume, papier;
Ce que nomme escry vistement. (*Testament*, 789-790)
(Hurry, get ink, pen, paper
Write down quickly what I dictate).

Je cuidé finir mon propos;
Mais mon ancre trouvé gelé. (*Lais*, 307-308)
(I tried to finish my task
But my ink was frozen).

[3] See, for example, Villon's use of *gros* in verse 286.

Chapter Nine

[1] See verse 47 of the *Lais*.

[2] It is Kuhn who originally suggested the reading of *mâle-ment* for *mallement*. He attaches the adverb to *mourant* instead of *espoignoit* and sees an act of sexual prowess in the death of the *povre Villon* (p. 333).

[3] I first proposed this interpretation in "The Povre Villon and Other Martyred Lovers of the *Testament*" (in *Neophilologus*, 64, 356).

[4] The religious symbolism to which I refer has only recently come to light. Jean-Charles Payen was the first to draw attention to this aspect of the closing ballad ("Le coup de l'étrier: Villon martyr et Goliard ou comment se faire oublier quand on est immortel?" in *Etudes Françaises* 16, 21-34). In a paper written before the publication of Payen's article and published slightly later, I examined the same evidence and drew similar conclusions ("The Conclusion of the *Testament*: An Image in the Shroud?" in *Fifteenth-Century Studies*, 5, 61-66).

[5] The fact that the word is consistently associated with the color black may be explained by its etymology. *Morillon* derives from the Old French *morel*, an adjective primarily applied to horses (*moreau* in modern French), and indicating a dark brown or black color, derived in turn from the vulgar Latin *maurellus*, a corruption of *Maurus*, originally designating a dark-skinned inhabitant of Africa. Given its history of linguistic associations with blackness, the word *morillon* appearing at the end of Villon's poem clearly conveys, among other things, an image of color. While the play on *mort-illon* has been pointed out by various critics (e.g. Kuhn 334, Thuasne III 548, Rychner II 275), the connotation of color, and the symbolic values attached to this connotation remain unexplored.

[6] See, for example, the *Dictionnaire des symboles* (Paris: Laffont, 1969).

Conclusion

[1] See Winthrop Rice, *The European Ancestry of Villon's Satirical Testaments* (New York, 1941).

[2] *Les testaments coutumiers au xve siècle* (Paris: Macon, 1903), p. 80.

SELECTED BIBLIOGRAPHY

I. Annotated Editions:

Rychner, Jean and Henry, Albert, ed. *Le Testament Villon*, 2 vols. Geneva: Droz, 1974. (The best annotated edition of Villon's poetry. Incorporates numerous advances in Villon scholarship subsequent to Thuane's edition of 1923.)

Thuasne, Louis, ed. *François Villon, Oeuvres*, 3 vols. Paris: Picard, 1923. (Still, sixty years after its publication, one of the most complete and enlightening commentaries of Villon's poetry. Especially strong in philological analysis; provides numerous examples of fifteenth-century French usage.)

II. Translations

Bonner, Anthony. *The Complete Works of François Villon*. New York: David McKay, 1960. (Somewhat flat compared to the Kinnell translation, but still useful.)

Kinnell, Galway. *The Poems of François Villon*. Boston: Houghton Mifflin, 1977. (A fairly faithful and highly readable translation by a well respected poet.)

III. Secondary Sources: Books

Anacker, Robert. *François Villon*. New York: Twayne Publishers, 1968. (An overview of Villon's work written primarily for those with no previous knowledge of fifteenth-century French literature. A good point of departure for further reading.)

Burger, André. *Lexique de la langue de Villon*. Geneva: Droz, 1957. (An indispensable research tool for any study of Villon's language.)

Champion, Pierre. *François Villon*. Paris: Champion, 1913. (Contains almost all known biographical data on the poet as well as interesting background information on fifteenth-century Paris and Villon's social milieu. Meticulously researched.)

Demarolle, Pierre. *L'Esprit de Villon*. Paris: Nizet, 1968. (A study of Villon's style including essays on his use of imagery, puns, and satire.)

-------- *Villon: un testament ambigu.* Paris: Larousse, 1973. (A synthesis of major critical work on Villon emphasizing the problems and complexities associated with the *Lais* and the *Testament.*)

Dufournet, Jean. *Recherches sur le Testament de François Villon*, 2 vols. (2nd edition). Paris: Société d'Edition d'Enseignement Supérieur, 1971. (Enlightening explications of selected passages from the *Testament.*)

-------- *Nouvelles recherches sur Villon.* Paris: Champion, 1980. (Further textual commentaries amplifying the critic's earlier work. Includes a synthesis of Tzara's theories on Villon's anagrams.)

-------- *Villon et sa fortune littéraire.* Bordeaux: Ducros, 1970. (Traces the literary influence and critical interest surrounding Villon's work from the 16th through the 20th century.)

Deroy, Jean. *François Villon: recherches sur le Testament.* The Hague: Mouton, 1967. (The transcription of a lecture in which Deroy analyzes several passages of the *Testament*, concluding with the hypothesis that Villon is the author of *Pathelin*.)

Fox, John. *The Poetry of Villon.* London: Thomas Nelson and Sons, 1962. (A well written introduction to Villon's work with special emphasis on the technical aspects of the poetry as well as syntax and vocabulary.)

Guiraud, Pierre. *Le Testament de Villon: ou le gai savoir de la basoche.* (The first chapter "L'identité des légataires" provides a useful summary identifying most of the heirs cited in the *Testament*.)

Kuhn, David. *La Poétique de François Villon.* Paris: Armand Colin, 1967. (A penetrating exploration of Villon's poetry full of erudition, perceptivity, and originality. A landmark in Villon criticism.)

LeGentil, Pierre. *Villon.* Paris: Hatier, 1967. (One of the most concise and useful introductions to Villon's work. Contains a synopsis of the *Lais* and the *Testament*, as well as thematic analyses.)

Petit-Morphy, Odette. *François Villon et la scholastique*, 2 vols. Paris: Champion, 1977. (An exhaustive examination of the relationship between Villon's poetry and medieval scholasticism.)

Rice, Winthrop H. *The European Ancestry of Villon's Satirical Testaments.* New York: The Corporate Press, 1941. (A study of the genre of the satirical testament in its Latin, French, and non-French vernacular forms.)

Rossman, Vladimir R. *François Villon: les concepts médiévaux du testament.* Paris: Jean-Pierre Delarge, 1976. (Examines the relationship between the medieval will and Villon's two poetic wills.)

Siciliano, Italo. *François Villon et les thèmes poétiques du moyen âge.* Paris: Colin, 1934. (A classic study elucidating the literary tradition underlying Villon's poetry. Tends to minimize the personal character of Villon's work.)

-------- *Mésaventures posthumes de Maître Françoys Villon.* Paris: Picard, 1973. (A defense of his earlier work and an attempt to refute certain recent trends in Villon criticism.)

Vitz, Evelyn Birge. *The Crossroads of Intentions: A Study of Symbolic Expression in the Poetry of François Villon.* The Hague: Mouton, 1974. (An imaginative approach to Villon's poetry, focusing on the *Testament,* and presenting a number of original and credible interpretations.)

IV. Secondary Sources: Articles

Bianciotto, Gabriel. "Troïle et Robert d'Estouteville," in *Mélanges offerts à Jean Frappier.* (Geneva: Droz, 1970), 115-132. (Examines the parallel between Robert d'Estouteville and Troïle (*Roman de Troïle*), and concludes that Villon was personally acquainted with Robert.)

Calin, William. "Observations on Point of View and the Poet's Voice in Villon," *L'Esprit Créateur,* 7 (1967), 180-187. (Focuses on the ambiguous nature of the narrator's persona in the *Testament.*)

Demarolle, Pierre. "Pour l'interprétation du texte de Villon," *Romance Notes,* 14 (1973), 613-620. (Examines the role of love and money in the "doctrine de la Belle Heaulmière"--verses 533-560.)

DuBruck, Edelgard. "Villon's Two Pleas for Absolution," *L'Esprit Créateur,* 7 (1967), 188-196. (Contains an enlightening explication of the "Ballade pour prier Nostre Dame.")

Frank, Grace. "The Impenitence of François Villon," *Romanic Review,* 37 (1946), 225-236. (Finds little evidence of contrition in Villon's poetry.)

-------- "Villon's Poetry and the Biographical Approach," *L'Esprit Créateur,* 7 (1967), 159-169. (Defends the study of Villon's work within a limited biographical context.)

Gothot-Mersch, Claudine. "Unité du *Testament* de Villon" in *Mélanges offerts à Rita Lejeune*, vol. 2. (Gembloux: J. Duculot, 1969), 1411-1426. (Rejects Siciliano's assertion that the *Testament* is a carefully structured work. Emphasizes spontaneity of the poem.)

Hayes, Joseph J. "Gothic Love and Death: François Villon and the City of Paris," *Journal of Popular Culture*, 11 (1978), 719-729. (Considers the role of the city in the *Testament*, Villon's fusion of courtly and popular literary tradition, and the elements of *eros* and *thanatos*.)

Henry, Albert. "Pour le commentaire des huitains V and VI du *Testament*," *Romania*, 88 (1967), 399-404. (Elucidates a difficult passage of the poem.)

Jacob, Alain-Guy. "Actualité de Villon" in *Mélanges offerts à Rita Lejeune*, vol. 2. (Gembloux: J. Duculot, 1969), 1427-1431. (Commentary on verses 169-170: "Je plains le temps de ma jeunesse...")

Lacy, Norris J. "The Flight of Time: Villon's Trilogy of Ballades." *Romance Notes*, 22 (1982), 353-358. (A fresh reading of the first three ballads of the *Testament*, emphasizing their thematic unity.)

-------- "Villon in His Work: the *Testament* and the Problem of Personal Poetry," *L'Esprit Créateur*, 18 (1978), 60-69. (A revealing examination of Villon's complex poetic personality. Questions whether Villon's poetry can actually be termed "personal" in the commonly accepted sense of the word.)

Lecoy, Félix. "Notes sur le texte ou l'interprétation de quelques vers du *Testament* de Villon," *Romania*, 80 (1959), 493-514. (Draws attention to several textual problems and suggests improvements to the Longnon-Foulet text.)

Lonigan, Paul R. "Villon's Triptych: Verses 329-412 of the *Testament*" *Neuphilologische Mitteilungen*, 70 (1969), 611-623. (Demonstrates the unity of Villon's famous trilogy of ballads which the author views as three panels of a "poetic triptych.")

Mela, C. "Je, Françoys Villon..." in *Mélanges offerts à Jean Frappier*. (Geneva: Droz, 1970) 775-796. (An interesting analysis of the *Testament* based partially on structuralist theory.)

Pallister, Janis L. "Attrition and Contrition in the Poetry of François Villon," *Romance Notes*, 11 (1969), 392-398. (Refutes Grace Frank's view of Villon as impenitent. Demonstrates the importance of theology in Villon's poetry.)

Pickens, Rupert T. "The Concept of the Feminine Ideal in Villon's *Testament*: Huitain LXXXIX," *Studies in Philology*, 70 (1973), 42-50. (A detailed analysis of the stanza introducing the "Ballade pour prier Nostre Dame.")

Poirion, Daniel. "L'Enfance d'un poète: François Villon et son personnage," in *Mélanges offerts à Mademoiselle Jeanne Lods* (Paris: Ecole Normale Supérieure de Jeunes Filles, 1978), 517-529. (An important study of the theme of childhood in Villon's poetry.)

-------- "Opposition et composition dans le *Testament* de Villon," *L'Esprit Créateur*, 7 (1967), 170-179. (Convincingly demonstrates that Villon's poem in structured on "la logigue de l'opposition.")

Sargent, Barbara Nelson. "On Certain Lines of Villon's *Testament*," *L'Esprit Créateur*, 7 (1967), 197-204. (Corrects several faulty passages of the Longnon-Foulet text.)

Spitzer, Leo. "Etude ahistorique d'un texte: Ballade des dames du temps jadis," *Modern Language Quarterly*, 1 (1940), 7-22. (Disputes Siciliano's claim that the ballad was composed prior to the *Testament*. A masterful *explication de texte*.)

Terdiman, Richard. "The Structure of Villon's *Testament*," *Publications of the Modern Language Association*, 82 (1967), 622-633. (Analyzes the poem's structure as a composite of four "thematic waves.")

Uitti, Karl D. "A Note on Villon's Poetics," *Romance Philology*, 30 (1976), 187-192. (Excellent analysis of the "Ballade pour prier Nostre Dame" and the "Ballade de la Grosse Margot.")

Vidal, Elie. "Villon et Robert d'Estouteville," *Studies in Philology*, 59 (1962), 31-40. (Questions the theory that Villon and Robert were well acquainted with each other.)

Wagner, R. L. "Lecture de Villon," in *Mélanges offerts à Jean Frappier* (Geneva: Droz, 1970), 1095-1101. (A commentary on verses 89-328 of the *Testament*.)

Weinmann, Heinz. "L'économie du *Testament* de François Villon," *Etudes Françaises*, 16 (1980), 35-61. (Discusses the implications of Villon's choice of the will as the form for his poem.)